GOLDILOCKS

GoLDiLocks

by

WALTER & JEAN KERR

Lyrics by Joan Ford, Walter and Jean Kerr

Doubleday & Company, Inc., Garden City, New York

Photographs by Friedman-Abeles

GOLDILOCKS was first presented by The Producers Theatre as a Robert Whitehead Production at the Lunt-Fontanne Theatre, New York City, on Saturday, October 11, 1958, with the following cast:

IN ORDER OF APPEARANCE

MAGGIE HARRIS	Elaine Stritch
GEORGE RANDOLPH BROWN	Russell Nype
MAX GRADY	Don Ameche
LOIS LEE	Pat Stanley
PETE	Nathaniel Frey
ANDY	Richard Armbruster
MAX'S ASSISTANTS	Gene Varrone, Sam Greene
J.C.	Martin Wolfson
BESSIE	Margaret Hamilton

Directed by Walter Kerr Settings by Peter Larkin
Dances and Musical Numbers Costumes by Castillo
  Staged by Agnes de Mille

Lighting by Feder

Music by Leroy Anderson
Lyrics by Joan Ford, Walter and Jean Kerr
Musical Director, Lehman Engel
Orchestrations by Leroy Anderson and Philip J. Lang
Dance Music arranged by Laurence Rosenthal
Production Associate, Joseph I. Levine

GOLDILOCKS

ACT I

Scene 1

We first see the lighted marquee of a New York theater, 1913. Outside the theater there are posters of a clown, obviously the principal comedian, and the leading lady, dressed in a garish red hussar's outfit. Signboards tell us that this is the farewell performance of a musical comedy called "Lazy Moon."

The marquee dissolves to what is going on inside: the finale of the show. Boldly painted wing-and-drop scenery. Three canoes are being paddled back and forth across a silvery sea. The BOYS wear period ice-cream suits, the GIRLS carry parasols. On the dock, downstage, the finale is being danced and sung by the CLOWN and the rest of the COMPANY.

COMPANY.   Johnny took his Jenny for a stroll in the park
One fine June night.
Jenny looked at Johnny and she said, "It's so dark—
Where's the moonlight?"
Johnny liked the dark 'cause he was feeling romantic,
Jenny wouldn't spark and it was driving him frantic.
At last he raised his head up and cried:

BOYS. Time to get up, you good-for-nothing Lazy Moon.
Upsy-daisy, moon!
Need your help to make my baby
Tell me "yes" instead of "maybe"
But before she will kiss me, baby wants her gold balloon.
Any sensible moon
Would know what I'm waiting for.
Be sensible, moon,
Whatcha so exasperating for?
It's after nine, so rise and shine,
You Lazy Moon.

The BOYS *plead with the* GIRLS.

Let's forget that moon, let us cuddle and spoon.

GIRLS. Oh, the wicked things you say!

BOYS. Let's discuss the size of the stars in your eyes.

GIRLS. Anybody for croquet?

BOYS. If I beg and tease and go down on my knees——

GIRLS. You can pick me up my glove——
There now, let the moon rise——

BOYS. Let it *soon* rise!
Heavens above—I love you!

Now the MOON *begins to rise over the water. The leading
lady is seated in its crescent.*

GIRLS. Time to get up, you good-for-nothing Lazy Moon.

BOYS, *singing an obbligato patter*. Shame on you, moon,
   blame on you, moon.
How can you be so persnickety?

GIRLS.   Upsy-daisy, moon!

BOYS.   This little romance is rickety.

GIRLS.   Need your help to make my baby
Tell me "yes" instead of "maybe."

BOYS.   Shine! Shine! Make her mine!

GIRLS.   But before she will kiss me, baby wants her gold
   balloon.

BOYS.   Buckle your shoe, let us skiddoo,
Leave us not have us no hullabaloo.

GIRLS.   Any sensible moon
Would know what I'm waiting for.
Be sensible, moon,
Whatcha so exasperating for?

BOYS.   Why, moon, why? Try, moon, try!

GIRLS.   It's after nine, so rise and shine,
You Lazy Moon!

*Voices swell to a finish and the act curtain—an olio drop
of the period—falls. It rises again immediately for a* COM-
PANY *bow, and then, as it starts to descend once more, the*
CLOWN *steps forward, putting up his hands and speaking
to the audience.*

CLOWN.   Thank you, thank you! You've been awfully good
to us. This is the last performance of "Lazy Moon" in New
York, and on Monday we're opening in Chicago. . . . But
we're all a little sad up here tonight . . . because we're
losing our girl in the moon. Come here, Maggie.

*The crescent has been lowered and the surprised leading
lady,* MAGGIE HARRIS, *is being escorted down to the foot-
lights.* CLOWN *takes her hand.*

Maggie's leaving us. I don't know why—she says she loves
the guy——

Squeals and handclaps from the CHORUS GIRLS.

I know he's around here somewhere—

Going toward the wings looking off.

—if he isn't, it'll be the first performance he's missed.

Gesturing off.

Come on, come on, they won't bite you!

GEORGE RANDOLPH BROWN *is urged on from the wings, reluctantly but pleasantly. The* CHORUS *breaks into encourag-
ing applause.*

Ladies and gentleman, I want you to meet the happy man,
Mr. George Randolph Brown.

GEORGE *bows nervously, grinning, as* CLOWN *draws him to*
MAGGIE, *joins their hands, begins singing the finale phrase
again.* FULL COMPANY *picks it up heartily.* MAGGIE *blows
kisses to the audience, while* GEORGE *remains sheepishly beside the* CLOWN, *attempting to join in song.*

Curtain comes down on end of song as MAGGIE *curtsies low to the audience. The curtain is now transparent so that we can see the scenery being dismantled and members of the* COMPANY *wishing* GEORGE *luck.*

Scene 2

At the same time MAGGIE'S *dressing room is moving into view. There are baskets of flowers everywhere.* MAGGIE'S MAID *and a chorus-girl* FRIEND *are helping her change into an evening dress.*

MAID. I'm really going to miss you, Miss Harris.

MAGGIE. And I'll miss you, too, Dolly. But I'm not going to miss that dirty cardboard moon or those silly canoes or this drafty dressing room.

FRIEND. I was sure you'd marry an actor.

MAGGIE. Actors don't marry, Patty. They sublet.

MAID. I must say your young man seems handsome—and they tell me he's very rich.

MAGGIE. Oh, George is rich, but with him it's not a disease. I'll tell you the kind of guy he is. On Christmas Eve he'll put the kids' tricycles together himself.

COMPANY *enters noisily from all sides to say goodbye.*

ACTOR, *in the pandemonium*. You *say* you're leaving the
theater. You'll be right back here in six months!

MAGGIE. Uh-uh! Not this kid!

FRIEND, *tearfully*. Oh, Maggie, I just never did honestly
think you'd go!

MAGGIE, *sings*.   No tears for me, boys,
 I'll tell ya what I'm goin' to be, boys—
 The perfect lady, the way I planned,
 So give the little lady a great big hand.

 Ragtime, I'm through now,
 No honky-tonk piano will do now.
 It's Bach for me at the baby grand
 So give the little lady a great big hand

 I'm through pretending!
 This ingenue has found
 Her happy ending,
 The trunk I was born in is attic-bound

 So-o-o-o—
 You take the gay time
 For me it's gonna be P.T.A. time.
 I've found my way to the promised land
 So give the little lady a great big wonderful hand

As her friends join in.

 Goodbye, goodbye to the day coach,
 To the grease paint, to the two-a-day.
 There's been a switch in the play, coach!
 When the whistle starts a-blowin'
 The lady is goin' away.
           Farewell, farewell,
 I'm gonna miss you less than I can say.

Members of the COMPANY *put on a lively, reminiscent vau-
deville show for* MAGGIE, *in which the* MAID *joins.*

COMPANY.   Ragtime, shoo now,
No honky-tonk piano will do now.
Now give that little fella a great big hand

To MAGGIE

No more pretending,
Your star's descending,
Hap-hap-happy ending.
Give that little lady a great big wonderful hand.

MAGGIE.   My star is set, boys,
I'll never shed a tear of regret, boys,
So send me off with a big brass band
And give the little lady—
I'm gonna be a lady—

COMPANY.   So give the little lady—

MAGGIE.   I wanna be a lady—

COMPANY.   So give the little lady a great big wonderful—

All join in rhythmic clapping.

—hand!

CHORUS BOY.   Hey, don't I get a goodbye kiss?

Clamor from the others as MAGGIE *whirls among the boys
and girls, kissing them quickly. During this,* MAX GRADY
*enters the dressing room, unnoticed, and—on a sudden turn
—*MAGGIE *kisses him, too.* MAX *holds onto her and makes
the most of it. The others have gone now.* MAGGIE *pulls
out of the kiss, backs away.*

MAGGIE.   Who are you?

MAX.   The name is Grady. Max Grady.

MAGGIE.   I'm sorry. The name doesn't mean anything to me at all.

MAX.   It will.

MAGGIE.   You get a big kick out of yourself, don't you?

MAX.   I'm all I have.

Now speaks briskly.

I don't want to keep you. Just be on the set tomorrow morning at six o'clock. You don't need a costume, but bring your own make-up.

Turns to go.

MAGGIE.   What are you talking about?

MAX, *turning back.*   I'm talking about a motion picture film called "Frontier Woman." Does that ring a bell anywhere? We start work tomorrow morning. I am the director, and you, I have reason to believe, are the leading lady.

MAGGIE'S *hands have gone to her face, as it all comes back to her.*

MAGGIE, *fast, affable, highhanded.*   Mr. Grady! How *could* that have gone out of my mind? You know, when I spoke to that poor man from your company, I naturally thought I'd be free. As it turns out, however, I'm going to be married—you may have heard of my fiancé, Mr. George Randolph Brown——

MAX, *exactly as gracious and affable, taking a contract out of his pocket.* And when I saw your name on this contract, I naturally thought I was going to have the pleasure of directing you. As it turns out, I'm going to have to bring you to court—you may have heard of my attorney, Mr. James Rothwell Stone——

MAGGIE. *You* are a mean, contemptible bully.

Quickly.

But you're not serious?

MAX, *nodding, with a vinegar smile.* That's what makes me so mean and contemptible.

MAGGIE, *shouting.* But I'm getting married in three weeks!

MAX, *also shouting, matching her tone precisely.* I don't expect to render you unfit!

MAGGIE. You get out of here! Take your horrible hat and get out of here! You can drag me into court for all I care!

MAX. Has it occurred to you that Mr. George Randolph Brown might care?

MAGGIE, *a pause as this registers.* How long would it take to make this stupid, dumb picture?

MAX. Five days.

MAGGIE, *screaming*.   Five days to make one of those idiotic, moronic little things that only run five minutes!

MAX.   This idiotic, moronic little thing is going to run ten minutes.

MAGGIE.   No, it's absolutely unthinkable. My trousseau isn't finished, I've got a dozen parties, I have to get my teeth fixed——

MAX.   I began life as a dentist. If there's any little thing I can do——

MAGGIE, *turning on him*.   Look, Doc—I have some reputation, I can't have my name on this thing!

MAX.   We won't use your name. We'll call you—

With a discreet little bow.

—Goldilocks.

MAGGIE.   I can't be mixed up with it!

MAX.   If you feel that way, why'd you sign the contract?

MAGGIE.   I signed the contract because I wanted the money. Now I don't want the money!

MAX.   All right, don't *take* the money!

MAGGIE.   I'll take it!

She sneezes suddenly.

MAX, *going to her swiftly*.   You haven't got a cold?

MAGGIE, *deadly sweet*.   I appreciate your solicitude, but no, I am not coming down with pneumonia. I said I'd be there and I'll be there.

An unexpected shout.

So what are you worrying about?

MAX.   You kissed me when I came in here. I might have caught it.

The door bangs open and GEORGE *enters, carrying the framed poster of* MAGGIE *in hussar's uniform we have seen earlier.*

GEORGE.   They were taking this down in the lobby, Maggie. I bought it for us.

MAGGIE, *appalled*.   George! Darling, you don't want that!

GEORGE.   *That* was the poster that first drew me into this theater. I was on my way to hear a Boccherini quartet——

Notices MAX.

Who's this?

MAX, *extending his hand*.   Boccherini. My phone isn't listed.

MAGGIE.   Mr. Grady, have I shown you this before? It's a door.

MAX, *going, but glancing chummily back at* GEORGE.   She's a sweet girl. Be good to her.

He goes.

MAGGIE, *turns to* GEORGE, *distraught and incoherent.* Oh, George, *think* of my signing that contract! I can't go up to Ten Oaks for five whole days. Your mother will think I'm afraid to meet her. I *am* afraid to meet her. Oh, George, I just don't deserve anybody as sweet and as good as you—

Non-stop.

—and you will get rid of that damn picture immediately!

GEORGE.   Not another word about that picture! It's you, and it's true and it's good and it's beautiful.

MAGGIE, *pouting.*   All right. Keep it. Hang it in the family gallery!

GEORGE.   I've said it before and I'll say it again. What my family needs is new blood.

MAGGIE.   But not all over the wall!

GEORGE *grins, puts his arm around her. She relaxes, a bit wistfully.*

George, I don't want to be like that. I want to be like the Browns. I really want to know which fork to use without looking at you first. I want to be on committees, and discuss the international situation, and wear dresses that are so unbecoming you just *know* they're right.

Sudden panic.

Oh, George, what if I'm a flop at it and everybody sees right through me and you're embarrassed for me and——

He silences her by kissing her. He sings.

GEORGE.   One good kiss, you know, deserves another
And another.
Do you mind?
I want to keep the first from being lonely
If you will only
Be so kind.

Tomorrow and tomorrow and tonight, if not before,
We'll meet and kiss
But tell me this—
Do you promise me there'll always be one more?

Kiss me for each star above,
One by one, but oh, my love,
Save a kiss against a cloudy sky.

Sweet and twenty kisses spend
But remember, daydreams end,
And a night may come when sweethearts sigh.

Let's make no mistake.
Loving hearts can break.
Put away
A rainy-day
Caress
Yes——

Kiss me dancing, kiss me still,
Kiss me now, but if you will,
Save a kiss to save me when I cry,
Save a kiss for bye and bye.

MAGGIE.   Let's make no mistake
GEORGE.   We're making no mistake
MAGGIE.   Loving hearts can break
GEORGE.   Our hearts will never break
MAGGIE.   Put away a rainy-day caress
GEORGE.   Yes——

MAGGIE.   Kiss me dancing, kiss me still
GEORGE.   Whisper this——
MAGGIE.   Kiss me now, but if you will
GEORGE.   Save a kiss
MAGGIE.   Save a kiss to save me when I cry
GEORGE.   Promise me that you will always
BOTH.   Save a kiss for bye and bye.

The lights fade.

Scene 3

MAX'S *studio, which is simply a fenced-in vacant lot in New York City, with the sky line beyond. A canvas painted to look like the wild West is stretched on poles before the sky line. In front of it a wilderness cabin is being assembled, open to view. This has two practical walls, several windows, a door. Various period props: a potbellied stove, poker, broom, cradle, chairs, a telegraph table and instrument, a clock painted on the wall. The painting is flat in the primitive manner of the period. Several* ACTORS *in Indian costume are idly playing cards.* PETE, *the cameraman, is moving camera into position.* MAX *enters swiftly.*

MAX. Try it over there, Pete. Andy, mark your sight lines.

To BESSIE, *the wardrobe woman.*

Miss Harris is due here any minute. Do you have a costume for her?

BESSIE. What kind of a costume?

MAX. Nothing stylish. Something backwoodsy—calico—shapeless——

BESSIE, *glancing at dress she has on, which fits the description almost perfectly.*   You're not going to get this one. Max, I can't stay around here sewing costumes. I have to get back to my farm.

MAX.   Forget about those chickens. They have each other.

Goes to camera.

BESSIE, *to passing* INDIAN.   Hey, Running Nose. Here's your blanket.

BESSIE *goes off through the fence, passing* LOIS, *who is young, sweet, earnest, and not very bright.*

LOIS.   Max, am I in this picture?

MAX.   No.

LOIS.   Max, why don't you put me in a picture?

MAX.   Because, my little peach blossom, you haven't one single shred of talent.

LOIS.   You say that just because I live around the corner and you're used to me. Why don't you take me seriously?

MAX.   Seriously, Lois, you're a very sweet girl. Now I have work to do.

LOIS.   Max, did you ever think of getting married?

MAX.   Certainly not. We Gradys never marry. That's why we're dying out.

LOIS. Well, I think it's all right, when you're young, not to be married. You'd miss all the fun. But what I worry about is when the children are grown up and gone, *then* shouldn't I be married?

MAX. Uh—what children are these?

LOIS. Can't you *have* children?

MAX. Well, not just now. I have all these people on salary, and——

MAGGIE *and* GEORGE *are arriving.*

MAGGIE. George, you don't really have to wait around for me——

GEORGE, *fascinated by the studio.* Say! This is interesting.

MAGGIE, *going to* MAX. I'm here.

MAX. I'm sorry I can't kneel. I have this trick knee.
Gesturing beyond fence.
The costume department is over here.
As she crosses him.
You look older in the daylight.

MAGGIE. I am twenty-six years old!

MAX. But it's been a hard twenty-six years, hasn't it?

Glaring at him, she lets him show her through the fence.

LOIS, *approaching* GEORGE, *who is studying the cabin.* Mr.
Brown? I was there at "Lazy Moon" last night when you
came on stage. I clapped.

GEORGE.   That was very kind of you. Are you a friend of Mr.
Grady's?

LOIS.   Well, how shall I put it? I'm chasing him.

GEORGE, *grinning.*   Are you catching him?

LOIS.   No. He's only interested in movies. But I'm very
tenacious. Around here they call me the tagalong kid.

GEORGE.   But what do you hope to get out of all this per-
sistence?

LOIS.   Max.

As MAX *is returning through fence, two of his* ASSISTANTS
*wheel in an enormous carved griffin from opposite side of
stage.*

1ST ASST.   Mr. Grady. This came!

MAX, *delighted.*   Ah! Bring it in and let me admire it.

PETE, *worried.*   Max, you're not buying more of that stuff!

BESSIE *returns.*

MAX.   Bessie! I just got myself a new piece of Egyptian scenery. What do you think of it?

BESSIE.   I think you should get another one and you'd have a swell pair of bookends.

MAX.   Bessie! I thought you were my friend. It's beautiful!

BESSIE, *pulling* MAX *aside*.   Max. You're not hiding any more of that stuff in my barn until you pay the rent.

MAX.   I've got to hide it somewhere.

BESSIE.   Listen. Eighteen months ago I made twenty-six cows homeless to get your Egyptian scenery into my barn. Since that time I have received one postcard from Asbury Park and, on my birthday, that necklace made of human hair. Now what I want to know is, what the hell?

MAX.   You'll get your rent.

ANDY *runs in, alarmed.*

ANDY.   Mr. Grady! We have a visitor!

MAX.   Who?

ANDY.   J.C.!

MAX, *quickly gesturing at griffin.*   Get that thing out of here before he sees it!

Another ASSISTANT *runs in, making anguished high signs.*

2ND ASST.   Max! J.C.!

MAX, *as the others rush griffin through fence.*   Hide it! Quick!

From the other side of the lot J.C. *appears in a wheel chair,*
snarling at the BOY *who is pushing him.* J.C. *is a small,*
wiry, completely tough elderly man, and he is accompanied
by a menacing ACCOUNTANT *with a briefcase.*

J.C., *to* BOY.   Will you watch what you're doing or do you
want to get another job?

MAX, *quickly affable.*   Hello, J.C.

J.C.   I have just one minute for you. I came into this thing
to make money. Instead of money I get involved statements
in which every other item is marked Miscellaneous Expenses.

MAX.   You'll get your money, J.C.

J.C.   I'm not getting it. Every picture that should make a
profit shows a loss. What's going on?

MAX.   You know how these things are.

Explaining, ticking it off on his fingers, a little worried.

The profits from "Mother Ferguson's Boy" we plowed into
"Destiny," the profits from "Destiny" we plowed into——

Interrupting himself before he has to explain too much.

Listen. I'll be starting another one on Friday and I'll need
a new leading lady. She's got to be able to wrestle a bear.

J.C.   I'll get you a leading lady on one condition. You get
me a complete financial statement. Okay?

MAX.   Certainly.

J.C., *to his* ATTENDANTS.   Let's go.

As he is being wheeled off he nearly runs down LOIS. *He stops to stare.*

I have a feeling I have come face to face with Miscellaneous Expenses.

J.C. *and* ATTENDANTS *go.*

PETE.   Max, you've got to stop buying this Egyptian stuff! Any minute now he's going to figure out where all the profits are going!

MAX.   Pete, I'm tired of ten-minute pictures. I'm going to be the first one in there with a big spectacle. And when I make Egypt, *everybody* gets paid!

MAGGIE *enters through fence, made up and in frontier costume.*

MAGGIE.   All right. Where's the dentist?

MAX, *swiftly into action.*   Company! Soldiers inside the telegraph station. Indians stand by.

To MAGGIE.

Do you know what this picture is about?

MAGGIE, *glancing at* INDIANS.   It's a baseball story.

MAX.   You're on the frontier. Muss your hair.

She does, a bit.

You've been trapped here for three days.

MAGGIE.   Oh. Three days.

Moves one more strand of hair.

MAX, *restraining himself, handing her prop baby gently.*
Your husband is dead. All you have in the world is your
baby. You look at him as though you could eat him.

*She raises baby in arms slightly. He puts out a restraining
hand.*

But you don't.

Takes her into position on set.

You're huddled against the wall. The Indians are attack-
ing. The men are holding them off and trying to telegraph
for help.

MEN *snap to positions. To* MAGGIE.

You're lonely, you're tired, you're terrified. You're cold,
pitifully cold.

Gestures to MUSICIANS, *who have one violin and one tom-
tom.*

Andy! Music!

Goes to camera position.

Begin.

Typical silent movie music. SOLDIERS *are firing out windows
of set. One shoots through a hole in the door.* INDIANS, *outside cabin, return firing.*

Telegraph operator! Stand up so I can see you!

TELEGRAPH OPERATOR *lurches up as though shot, staggers a
few feet, falls.*

Ben, now you try to get the message through!

One of SOLDIERS *runs to instrument as others quickly shift window positions to cover.*

And—you're shot!

BEN *staggers violently, reels, and falls.* MAX *now calls to* SOLDIER *standing at window directly above* MAGGIE.

Harry, you take his place! Go over to the table!

MAGGIE.   I wouldn't, Harry. It's a death trap.

HARRY *runs to table.*

MAX.   You reach out to touch it—

Shot.

—and you're gone!

MAGGIE.   Just a boy, too!

HARRY, *wearing a large coonskin cap, falls near* MAGGIE; *she grabs the hat and uses it as a muff.*

MAX.   What the hell are you doing that for?

MAGGIE, *turning toward him and shouting.*   It's cold, piti-fully cold!

MAX.   *Cut!*

Everything stops. MAX *crosses slowly, patiently to* MAGGIE.

Miss Harris, there are two things we do not do around here. We do not look into the camera—

Points at it, helpfully, then, with a sudden switch of tone, snatches the cap out of her hand.

—and we do not strip the dead!

Hurls hat at HARRY, *calls to cameraman.*

We'll clip that last bit and start with Harry!

HARRY *on his feet in position.*

Go!

Music and action. HARRY *staggers and falls again.*

Frank, start backing away from the windows. Keep shooting, keep shooting—you reach out to touch the instrument —*and*—you stagger——

FRANK *is shot and starts to stagger; he drops his gun and begins to clutch wildly at the furniture, going into a long death agony without falling. After a moment* MAGGIE *is heard.*

MAGGIE.   This picture is going to run more than ten minutes.

Finally FRANK *falls, but it is not over yet; kneels up, falls; raises his head, struggling; head down, his hands still come up, clawing.*

What is our attitude toward mercy killing?

FRANK *dies.*

MAX.   All right, the men are all gone now. The woman must take over. Get up. Put the baby down—gently, gently. Pray for strength.

MAGGIE *postures all this in the technique of the period.*

Square your shoulders. Pick up a gun. Go to the window. Shoot!

She fires a couple of shots.

Go to the table. You've got to send the message. Start sending.

She taps once, then pauses; he shouts.

What are you waiting for?

MAGGIE, *also shouting, but face up, not looking at camera.* I'm trying to keep it under ten words!

MAX *leaps out of his chair, angry, as she plunges back into business of sending.*

MAX.   Dammit, you send that message! Send it! Send it! Send it!

INDIAN *appears in window.*

Turn around! There's an Indian. Raise the gun. Shoot.

MAX *paces violently, driving the scene; she shoots and IN-DIAN falls; as she starts to turn back, another INDIAN takes his place.*

Window! Window! Start to shoot! The gun is empty. Show me the gun is empty! All right, whack him with it!

She hurls herself at INDIAN in window, hitting him with butt of gun; INDIAN and gun go out the window. Another IN-DIAN's hand is coming through hole in door toward latch.

The door!

MAGGIE *sees hand, grabs it and bites it. Scream as INDIAN disappears. Another is now at the lower window.*

Grab something. The poker. The poker from the stove!

She grabs poker and drives it into INDIAN, *pushes both through window.*

Back to the table! You've got to get the message through!

INDIAN *coming in upper window.*

Window! Window!

As she looks about for a weapon.

You're gonna hit him with the chair!

She grabs chair and smashes it to splinters on INDIAN'S *head. Meantime, a fresh* INDIAN *has retrieved her poker from dead* INDIAN *outside and is coming in lower window with it.*

They're coming from all sides!

She sees INDIAN *and snatches poker from him.*

MAGGIE.   That's my poker!

She hits INDIAN *in lower window with it, bashes* INDIAN *in upper window, and turns in time to whack* INDIAN *coming through door, a triple play. The last* INDIAN *somersaults forward from the blow and nearly crashes into the camera, but is tackled by* 1ST ASST. *before any damage can be done. New* INDIAN *in lower window.*

MAX.   He's going to get in! Grab something. The broom! Hit him with the broom!

MAGGIE, *harassed, having a terrible time getting through bodies and debris.*   I'm coming. I'm coming.

She snatches the broom and as she clambers over the

bodies one of the presumably dead SOLDIERS *lifts his head
and arm. She brushes him down with the broom.*

Die, will you!

She hits INDIAN *in window with the broom as another* IN-
DIAN *starts coming in the door.*

MAX.   Barricade the door!

*She tries to barricade the door by tipping over the table
but the feet of a dead* SOLDIER *are in the way.*

MAGGIE.   Move your feet!

All dead SOLDIERS *move their feet. She flings the table on
its side against the door and engages in a tug of war with*
INDIAN *outside. Now more* INDIANS *are coming from everywhere.*

MAX.   They're getting ahead of you. You're not working fast
enough! Come on, come on, come on! He's practically in
the room! Grab something! Hit him with something! Come
on! HIT HIM!

MAGGIE *snatches up the baby and whams it over the nearest*
INDIAN'S *head, blowing the baby to smithereens.*

Everything stops dead. Silence. MAX *walks slowly downstage. Then he roars to assembled group.*

Will you all have the decency to leave this bereaved
mother to me?

All scurry, including PETE *and* ASSISTANTS. MAX *turns to*
MAGGIE, *who expects an explosion. Instead, he now speaks
casually.*

Come here.

MAGGIE *puts what is left of the baby in the crib and walks slowly toward* MAX, *who doesn't quite look at her.*

This is junk, isn't it? I think probably a lot of people get a kick out of it, but it's junk. Still, I have to do it. I have to sneak just enough money out of each one of these things to build up a little pile for—something I want to do very much. And any day I lose in fun and games gets me in trouble.

Turning his attention to her.

You're in a tough spot, too. You're getting married and you want to get out of here. Now you can make wisecracks, and I can insult you. But that won't help either of us, will it?

MAGGIE, *wind out of her sails.*   No.

MAX.   Then what if we say the hell with it, and go to work?

MAGGIE, *struggles for a word, then makes up her mind.* All right.

MAX, *turning away and roaring to offstage* COMPANY.   *On* the frontier!

MAGGIE, *returning to work as the others stream in.*   I'll need another baby——

War whoops begin again and the lights cross-fade to:

Scene 4

The high board fence outside MAX's *studio. Work is over for the day and, in the twilight, members of the* COMPANY *are hurrying to get out of costume.* MAX *is slipping into his coat when* PETE *catches up with him.*

PETE.   Max, what am I gonna do about the daily payroll?

MAX.   How much money we got?

PETE.   One hundred and thirty-eight dollars. As I see it, we can pay either the soldiers or the Indians.

MAX.   Pay the Indians. They've had a rotten deal in this country.

MAGGIE *comes through a door in the fence, thoroughly disheveled.*

MAGGIE.   I'm exhausted! Look. Tomorrow could I be a soldier? I want to get shot and lie around all day like everyone else.

Sizing up MAX, *who looks reasonably dapper.*

It must be awfully tough on you . . . that soft fanny on that hard camp chair all day.

MAX, *tapping his forehead.*   It's the mental work that gets you. Don't think I wouldn't rather pitch in and have fun with the rest of you boys and girls. And let me tell you this —on the heights, it's pretty lonely.

MAGGIE.   How is it down there on the poop deck?

MAX.   Naturally, you want to know how your work has been. I think you can hope. I think there's a place for you here. You know, I keep my leading ladies for years.

Slipping his arm around her.

MAGGIE, *slipping right out.*   If you *don't* mind . . .

MAX.   Don't try to explain. You think I don't understand, but I do. You're fighting something. You feel yourself drawn to me—it's just simple chemistry—and you're fighting it. *Go on* fighting it!

MAGGIE, *stares at him, openmouthed, for a second.*   After that stuff begins to wear off, how do you feel—depressed, nervous?

She sings.

I am told you have admirers by the dozen,
I am sure you lead them all a merry dance.
What a blow when they discover
You have found the perfect lover,
When they realize they just don't have a chance. . . .

Other hearts may flutter when they see you passing by,
Others turn to butter every time they hear you sigh.
Me, I love the lovelight in your beady little eye
But no one'll ever love you like you do.

MAX.   Some go all to pieces when they see that girlish grin,
Some could write a thesis on the texture of your skin.
I adore the dimple in that small, receding chin
But no one'll ever love you like you do.

MAGGIE.   I can see this is no casual affair.

MAX.   When did you first begin to care?

MAGGIE.   Were you childhood sweethearts,
Did you stand beneath a tree
With a heart carved on it
And "I love me"?

MAX.   Mighty armies slumber with your picture by their
beds,
An imposing number kiss the ground your slipper treads.
Then there's me, I've saved a curl from both your little
heads——

BOTH.   But no one'll ever love you,
No, no one'll ever love you,
No, no, no one'll ever love you
Like you do!

BLACKOUT

Scene 5

MAX's *lot, about noon on the fifth day. In a two-second swirl of action, the* COMPANY *rides into a stirring melodramatic tableau, with* MAGGIE *and baby astride a cannon sur-rounded by dead* SOLDIERS *and a flag flying over them. It is obviously the end of the picture.*

PETE, *relaxing at camera.* The—End!

ANDY, *running forward to collect props.* Anybody who's in the bear picture get into your costume!

1ST ASST. We start in fifteen minutes!

MAGGIE, *disentangling herself from flag and coming down to* MAX. I didn't want to interrupt you while you were work-ing, but now that we're through, would you mind explain-ing the plot?

MAX, *grins.* When it's cut and put together, it makes sense in a weird way. You'd be surprised.

MAGGIE. Where do you go to see these things?

MAX.   Oh, there's a nickelodeon right next to the Fish Market.

Quickly.

Now tell me that's a good spot for it.

MAGGIE.   That's not fair! I've been very sweet and co-operative. Haven't I?

MAX.   Yes, we haven't lost a baby in a couple of days. Why should I kid you? You can act and you know it.

MAGGIE.   A tribute from the master!

2ND ASST., *hurrying through.*   Miss Harris. Mr. Brown called. He'll pick you up in ten minutes.

MAX.   Good luck.

Offers MAGGIE *his hand; they shake on it. As* MAGGIE *starts for dressing quarters,* LOIS *approaches her hesitantly.*

LOIS.   Miss Harris, I really don't know you well enough to ask you this—but since you're leaving today I'm not going to know you any better. Would you do me a favor?

MAGGIE.   Sure, Lois. What?

LOIS.   I'm going to sing tonight at the Fat Cat——

MAGGIE.   Fat Cat?

LOIS.   It's a roof garden.

MAX, *looking up from film* PETE *has brought him.*   Why, Lois! You're employed!

LOIS.   I'm not exactly employed. They're going to try me out.
It's a very tough place. Sometimes they don't even let you
finish—but I'm going to start.

MAGGIE.   And you'd like me to come and see you? Why, sure,
Lois.

Going.

I know George would enjoy it, too.

MAGGIE *disappears through fence and* LOIS *gives* MAX *a
haughty sniff as she passes him.*

PETE, *to* MAX.   You got a scenario for this next picture?

MAX, *handing* PETE *the film and taking a pencil and an
old envelope out of* PETE'S *pocket.*   I will have in three
minutes.

PETE.   They want fifty bucks for the bear outfit.

MAX.   Sell the Indian costumes.

PETE.   They're not ours.

MAX.   Then sell 'em for less. We can afford to take a loss.

1ST ASST.   Do we need a baby for this one?

MAX.   Yeah . . . and a bigger one. When the bear picks it
up in his teeth, I want to *see* it. Andy, we've got a rocking
chair?

ANDY *nods.*

Get me the old mountain background. And one real tree.

PETE. How can we start? Our new leading lady hasn't shown up yet.

MAX, *writing his scenario on the back of the envelope.* Call J.C.

PETE. I don't want to talk to J.C.! He expected you to send him a financial statement.

MAX. No, he didn't. He knows I can't add.

PETE *goes off in despair.* BESSIE *has been hovering, waiting her chance.*

BESSIE. Max, I want to make you a proposition.

MAX. Bessie! I have dreamed of this moment.

BESSIE. Max, be serious! We could both get out of all this. As the man on the street will tell you, Florida is the future.

MAX. Florida?

BESSIE. Now I have a chance to buy a big, wet piece of the future. Eight hundred acres of the most desirable swamp-land you ever saw——

ANDY, *entering with a large prop tree in his hand.* Mr. Grady. How's this?

MAX. Fine.

BESSIE, *persisting.* But I can't swing it alone, Max. I need someone like you—young, and eager, and slippery——

MAX. Thanks, Bessie. I'm needed here.

BESSIE. Max, this is kid stuff. Look at it—kid stuff! We could clear half a million in two years.

MAX, *pauses, then speaks directly.* Bessie, I wouldn't tell this to anybody but you. Someday I'm going to make a good picture.

PETE *returns, his face grim.*

MAX. Did you get J.C.?

PETE. I got him.

MAX. And?

PETE. We can't make the bear picture.

MAX, *showing a shade of real concern.* Why not?

PETE. You didn't get him that statement. He didn't get you a leading lady. He'll clean up the bills on "Frontier Woman" but that's it.

MAX. You mean he's really pulling out?

PETE. Right. We're through.

MAX. Let's not panic. Wait a minute. I've got it.

PETE. But he *said*——

MAX. He said he'd clean up the bills on "Frontier Woman." All right. We keep on making "Frontier Woman."

PETE, *insistent.*   We haven't got a leading lady!

MAGGIE, *popping in through fence.*   Bessie! I need help. My clothes must be mixed up with wardrobe and I have to get out of here!

MAX, *before* MAGGIE *can follow* BESSIE *off, in an innocent tone.* Miss Harris—you're not leaving?

MAGGIE.   Certainly I'm leaving.

MAX, *quite plausibly.*   But we haven't done the flashback.

MAGGIE.   Flashback?

MAX.   Yes. Where your grandmother fights with the bear.

MAGGIE.   My grandmother? What bear?

MAX, *very matter-of-fact.*   It's fifty years earlier. She's out in the wilderness. A bear steals her baby——

MAGGIE.   My, she *does* have her hands full. What's it to me?

MAX.   You are the grandmother.

MAGGIE.   And you are the funniest boy in the fifth grade. My contract says five days, we have now had five days of jolly companionship—goodbye!

MAX.   Your contract says nothing about five days. It says when the picture is finished.

MAGGIE.   But *you* said five days——

MAX.   *I said*——

MAGGIE.   Never mind! I don't want to hear it. I don't want to be drawn into your little daydreams. I have fought the good fight, I have killed every live Indian west of the Mississippi, and now you can go get yourself another girl!

MAX.   I couldn't get another girl if I wanted to! Where would I find a two-fisted Amazon who could work with a bear?

Her jaw drops. A pause.

MAGGIE.   Whistle me that again.

MAX.   Dear, you don't think I hired you for your dainty ways?

Putting up his hand.

I know, you're joining the caviar and crumpet set. You're going to pour tea, ride to the hounds, and sleep on thirteen mattresses. Bully, I say. But let's look life in the face, dear. You are a rough-and-tumble, hale and hearty big broth of a girl who will never be mistaken for the lady of the manor and who'll be kicking it up with the boys when you're a hundred and three!

She slaps him across the face, hard, and strides to the dressing quarters.

PETE.   I thought you handled that beautifully.

MAX.   Andy!

ANDY.   Yes, Mr. Grady?

MAX, *dropping into a chair.*   Where can we get a lawyer?

ANDY.   I don't think we can. We're known.

ANDY sits down, too.

PETE, *joining them, a morose trio.*   I've saved the best for last. J.C. has his own team of auditors going over the books. We're going to be better known.

GEORGE enters from the street side of the lot, cheerfully, ready to take MAGGIE off to Ten Oaks.

GEORGE.   Hello, there! I've come to pick up my girl. Since this was her farewell performance, I hope she was good.

MAGGIE, *hearing his voice and hurrying in.*   George?

Scurrying past the seated trio.

Come on!

GEORGE.   You're not leaving like this—in your costume?

MAGGIE, *impatient to go.*   Yes, I'm leaving like this in my costume and I hope they sue.

GEORGE.   Oh, has there been a row?

Glancing at MAX.

MAX.   Well, we're in the *middle* of the picture and Miss Harris is behaving as though she didn't have a contract.

GEORGE.   *Do* you have a contract?

MAGGIE. Oh, I have a contract. What I should have is a gun. We'll miss the train——

GEORGE. But if you leave now, does that create a problem for Mr. Grady?

MAGGIE. George, his problem began when he was born. He was in this jar, and they let him out——

GEORGE. Maggie——

MAGGIE, *shrill*. What are we standing here for?

GEORGE. A contract is the same as giving your word.

MAGGIE. George, always remember this. My word is worthless.

His face falls.

Oh, now I've done it. Something is burning inside you—what is it?

MAX, PETE, *and* ANDY *listen attentively, hopefully now.*

GEORGE. The great Brown family has had its share of drunks and no-goods, but there's never been one of us that didn't keep his promise. I told you the *famous* story about Commodore Brown. He made the family fortune trading with the Huron Indians. He gave them muskets and whiskey, and they gave him beaver pelts. Then, in 1780, he was living in a little town called Saginac. He had already received his pelts, and he had promised the Chief he would deliver the guns on the first day of the full moon. On the night *before* the full moon the Hurons attacked the village, killed all the men, and captured the women. But the next day, in spite of everything, he delivered those guns to the Hurons. He was much criticized.

MAX, PETE, *and* ANDY *rise and drift upstage, getting things ready for the picture.*

Honey, I hate to sound like a fanatic, but I guess *I* think it's important, too.

MAGGIE, *hands over her eyes.* You mean you think I should stay here and finish this dreary thing——

GEORGE. Worse than that, I can't even stay with you. Mother says I *have* to go to Ten Oaks tonight, to settle the wedding plans. Naturally, she thought we'd *both* be coming——

ASSISTANTS *are sliding mountain background into place behind* MAGGIE.

MAGGIE. I have to stay here, and I have to stay here alone!

GEORGE. Honey, I'll be back the minute I can. You're not mad at me?

MAGGIE, *as* GEORGE *kisses her goodbye.* No, no, no, no——

Almost upon GEORGE's *departing heels,* ANDY *places a baby on the ground before mountain background. An* ACTOR *dressed as a* BEAR *enters and receives instructions from* MAX. *In effect,* MAGGIE *is being quietly surrounded by the picture.*

MAX, *to* BEAR. Now, Frank, you've already stolen the baby. You paw it around a little——

BEAR *nods, drops to all fours, and starts to paw the baby*

while MAGGIE *stands stunned by the situation she finds herself in.*

Now you see the woman. She stands there rigid, paralyzed with fright.

BEAR *pulls at* MAGGIE's *skirt. She whips it away in anger.*

Rear on your hind legs. You start to maul her.

BEAR *gets his arms around* MAGGIE *but she dodges him, outraged. The* BEAR *mauls her again, more vigorously.*

The woman starts to come out of her trance—she does the only thing she can do—she—she——

MAGGIE, *forced to it, drives a swift upper to the* BEAR's *jaw. He drops.*

PETE, *to* MAX, *stopping the camera.*   Very unusual shot, don't you think?

MAX *nods, wryly.*

Are we supposed to think she killed the bear?

MAX.   No, she just stunned him. He dies of humiliation.

MAGGIE *suddenly drops to her knees beside the* BEAR, *who hasn't stirred.* ANDY *and* 2ND ASST. *enter.*

MAGGIE.   Frank, are you all right? Wait a minute! I think he *is* out!

MAX.   Water!

ANDY *hurries out for water as* MAX *kneels beside* BEAR.

MAGGIE. Help me with his head!

They get the bear head off.

Are you *sure* you're all right?

FRANK *nods, a bit groggily, as* ANDY *returns with a bucket of water.*

I'm sorry. I didn't have to take it out on you.

While they are helping the BEAR *to his feet and* MAGGIE *is wiping his face with a sponge,* MAX *takes the bear head to* PETE, *fascinated.*

MAX. Look at that. She snapped off a lower bicuspid.

PETE. I keep forgetting you were a dentist.

MAX. Never forget. It's the clue to my whole personality.

MAX *returns the bear head and offers* MAGGIE *a rocking chair, grinning and with a certain admiration. To* MAGGIE.

Sit down, champ. The crowd was with you. I thought the footwork was good, you kept your hands high, but before you go for the title, you'd better trim off a little weight.

MAX *goes through fence.*

BEAR, *glancing at* MAGGIE *as she sinks into rocker, disconsolate.* Hey, you look worse than I do. What's the matter?

MAGGIE. Well, it's all very simple. There was this Commodore Brown. He sold beaver pelts. So I'm stuck here by myself.

She sings.

When Goldilocks went visiting the bears
They came home from the forest unawares,
Found cushions off the chairs,
Porridge everywheres,
And bedlam in the bedroom when they hurried up the
    stairs.

When I come home I look around and sigh.
Everything is neat as apple pie,
A charming little nest!
It gets me so depressed
I want to die.
Know why?

Who's been sitting in *my* chair?
Just me. Just me.
Seems such a pity when I'd share
It willingly.
I want a den that is happy, homey,
I've got a yen for a lap below me.
If you were sitting in my chair—
Oh, gosh. Oh, gee.

Who's been eating my porridge?
Just me. That's who.
I'm just the type to go foraging for a midnight snack for
    two.
When you don't see a soul with your morning coffee
You can't casserole and you can't pull toffee.
If you were eating my porridge—
Oh, dear. Oh, do.

Heigh ho, and lackaday!
A lack of love will turn me gray.
I'd like to run away—just like Goldilocks——

Who's been sleeping in my bed?
Just me. Just *moi*.
I'd like a two-fisted biped
For my boudoir,
I'd like a tweed hanging next to that dress,
I'd like to need a larger mattress.
If you were sleeping in my bed—
Tra-la. Tra-la. Tra-la. Tra-la. . . .

BEAR *puts the head on, bows politely to* MAGGIE, *and they join hands for a little danced version of the song, together. By the end of it* MAGGIE *is feeling a bit more like herself. She is sitting on the* BEAR's *lap as* MAX *returns, swinging in briskly.* BEAR *kisses* MAGGIE's *hand and leaves.*

MAX. Come on. I'll take you to dinner.

MAGGIE. Cool off.

MAX. It's all right. We'll go halfies.

MAGGIE. Beat it.

MAX. What's the matter—you scared?

MAGGIE. Scared? Of what?

MAX. I know you're committed to George—but you don't want to deny yourself *all* pleasure.

As she opens her mouth to speak.

I know what you're going to say. I need a haircut. But I've got something.

MAGGIE, *suddenly, like a mother to a child.*   Come here.

He does.

Sit down.

He does.

Kiddo, what you've got is what I'm trying to get rid of. You represent what I've been surrounded by all my life. You are a common, on-the-make, hustler.

She has said this slowly and simply, letting it sink in. By the look on MAX's *face, we can see that he is actually stung.*

MAX, *quietly.*   Yeah?

MAGGIE.   Yeah. And I couldn't fall for you if you were the only living thing on the beach.

She turns her chair away.

He rises, circles.

MAX.   I'll pick you up at nine.

MAGGIE.   For what?

MAX.   You haven't forgotten you promised Lois you'd go to the Fat Cat?

MAGGIE.   Oh. I'll manage. I've got bus fare.

MAX.   That place is full of low, common hustlers. You'll be better off if you're with one you know.

MAGGIE.   Look. When I succeed in insulting you, will you tell me about it?

MAX, *squaring off with her.*   I don't think you can do it. I think you're strictly a one-punch girl, like with the bear. If you had to go three rounds with somebody your own size, I think you'd wilt.

MAGGIE, *accepting the challenge.*   Okay. Let's go three rounds. Nine o'clock.

As she is going through the fence.

Don't dress. I want to be able to recognize you.

PETE *returns, cleaning up props.*

MAX.   Pete, have I ever told you you have a noble brow and fine, intelligent eyes?

PETE.   Many times. Now what do you want?

MAX.   I want to be able to use Huckleberry Island starting Saturday.

PETE.   What for?

MAX, *thinking it out.*   It'll be a real nice place to shoot the pirate-girl flashback.

PETE.   The pirate girl?

MAX.   Yeah. The one in the boat.

PETE.   Oh. There's a boat.

MAX, *as though this were old stuff*.   Sure. The woman is cap
tured by pirates.

PETE.   Wait a minute. We're out in the wild West—Indians
—bears——

MAX, *warming to the improvisation*.   Right! The woman is
alone—on top of this mountain—she's sent up a smoke signal—now she's waiting—waiting——

PETE.   For the *Robert E. Lee?*

MAX.   She's about to despair. Then she has a dream. About
her grandmother. It makes her think.

PETE.   It makes us all think.

MAX, *glancing where* MAGGIE *has gone off*.   And Miss Harris
will be charming in all of it.

PETE.   Max, you can't keep her here *forever!* You developing
a sudden interest?

MAX.   Never. I'm not her type. You know me—I'm a common,
on-the-make, hustler.

PETE.   You're sweet. Don't let them spoil you.

PETE *goes, looking back curiously at* MAX.

MAX, *sings*.   Common—she says!
On the make—she says!
What I'll never take is the cake—
She says.

Lady, you shouldn't-a gone and told me what you told me.
Didn't you know you'd go and make me mad?
Tellin' a man he isn't man enough to care for—
That's bad.
Because there never was a woman
Who couldn't be had.

Maybe I'm not the kind of fancy Dan you go for.
Matter of fact, I like a noisy plaid.
Matter of fact, you'd never take me for no high-tone
College grad.
Still there never was a woman
Who couldn't be had.

Tell me I'm mean, green, oughta be kept in quarantine
And I'll never bat an eye.
Say that I'm crass, brass, certain to go to the foot of the
      class
And you'll never make me cry—
But when you tell me I could never make you tingle,
Lady, look out—I'm not Sir Galahad,
Lady, look out, I'm just an ordinary homespun low-down
      cad.
You see, there never was a woman
Who couldn't be had . . .
Be had . . .
Be had.

BLACKOUT

Scene 6

*The Fat Cat. A roof-garden jazz spot of the period, down-
town, very garish and going at full clip. We are just in
time for* LOIS' *number. She sings.*

LOIS.   When I pick my pussy foot up
Each lovin' Tom along the fences senses somep'n' new.
When I put my pussy foot down
Each happy feline makes a beeline to play peekaboo.
I cannot but observe
I touch a certain nerve,
I cause a small disturbance in the town
When I pick my pussy foot up
And I put my pussy foot down. . . .

Tiger cats
Tip their hats,
Flip their whiskers and purr.
Pekinese
Tell their fleas,
"Fellas, fellas, it's her!"
It don't behoove a lady to lie,
There is no other pussy like I.
Struttin' down the alley . . .
Debonair,

Nose in air,
I am rather a wow.
Such a dish,
So delish,
You may wish to meow.
I thought that sexy whistle was very pleasantly put
And won't you join me doin' the—
Come on, don't dally, doin' the—
Let's get the alley doin' the—
Pussy Foot!

There is a frenzied dance during which LOIS *barely manages to hold her own. When it is over, we discover* MAX *and* MAGGIE *at a side table.*

MAX.   I imagine you started out in a place like this. If you have the urge to get up and sing, don't consider my feelings.

MAGGIE.   Listen, I've seen this side of your character. I was expecting something *special* tonight. When do I get swept off my feet? I thought we'd wind up running barefoot through the park, like two happy children, working up *such* an appetite for those scrambled eggs at Childs'.

MAX, *sudden decision.*   Look. Don't come tomorrow.

MAGGIE.   Huh?

MAX.   Call your friend George and tell him you'll be joining him.

MAGGIE, *slight pause, head cocked.*   I know I'm slow—but I thought we were in the middle of a flashback.

MAX.   That wasn't a flashback. It's a whole new picture you're making. Your contract was up.

MAGGIE.   I knew it was up!

MAX, *nodding*.   I double-crossed you. And what's more I was going to add another whole sequence about a pirate girl and make you do that one, too. Or *try*.

MAGGIE.   Boy! You are the gem of the ocean. But why?

MAX.   That's easy. All my money comes from a sharp little crook in a wheel chair who has announced that "Frontier Woman" is my last picture. You can understand why I wanted to make "Frontier Woman" one of the *longest* pictures ever made.

MAGGIE.   No, I don't. There must be somewhere else you could get the money.

MAX.   Yeah, but that's only part of the story. The day I finish and the accounts are added up there is going to be a small discrepancy of sixteen thousand dollars.

MAGGIE, *slight pause*.   Wow. That's a lot of money.

MAX.   I've got a lot of scenery to show for it. Egyptian stuff. I've been collecting it for two years.

MAGGIE.   Why don't you just turn in the scenery?

MAX.   I'd rather go to jail.
Quite sincerely.
You should see my scenery. It's beautiful.

MAGGIE, *genuinely puzzled now*.   But I don't get it! If you want to keep making this picture, why are you letting me go?

MAX, *turning away*.   I said you could go. Do I have to give a reason?

MAGGIE.   Yes. You do. Now I'm curious!

MAX.   All right. Brace yourself. I find myself getting interested in you. And that won't do. In the first place I'd never make the grade, as you so clearly pointed out this afternoon. And in the second place I don't want to. I don't want to get involved.

MAGGIE.   Well, well, well! When you break down you really tell all, don't you?

MAX.   Yeah. Now let me put you in a cab.

Rises to go.

MAGGIE.   Wait a minute. What *are* you going to do?

MAX.   That, my dear, is not your problem.

MAGGIE, *insistent*.   But wait a minute! Just supposing I was willing to make this pirate sequence——

MAX.   Forget it.

MAGGIE.   It would at least give you three or four days to stall this guy—to raise some money——

MAX *silent*.

Look. It won't kill me to do it. And I promise you—you're
perfectly safe with me.

Decisive.

Now if we're going to start at six in the morning, let's get
out of here. I'll get my coat.

MAGGIE *off.* PETE *appears from around the bar, as though
he had been waiting.*

PETE, *quietly.*   It's okay about Huckleberry Island. Did you
talk her into the pirate sequence?

MAX.   No, she talked me into it. It was one of my finest
performances.

MAX *goes after* MAGGIE. *As* PETE *turns,* LOIS *appears from
bar.*

LOIS.   Why is Max going out with Maggie?

PETE.   Don't worry, kid. It's just business.

PETE *goes.*

LOIS.   It doesn't look like business to me.

LOIS *sits wistfully at table and sings a forlorn little reprise
of The Pussy Foot. Lights fade.*

Scene 7

Huckleberry Island, a few days later. The prow of a wrecked ship juts forward from the downstage wings. Upstage there is a lighthouse with a spiral staircase wrapped around it. Water and sky beyond. Swarming down the lighthouse steps and all over the ship are dueling PIRATES. PETE *is trailing them as fast as he can with his camera,* MAX *at his side, shouting directions. The battle gradually focuses on the ship, where* MAGGIE *appears, a pirate baby tucked under one arm. She is wearing a pirate costume—bandana, eye patch—and gradually decimating her pirate enemies. The scene ends with* MAGGIE *at the mast, triumphant. As soon as* MAX *gives the signal that the sequence is over,* BESSIE *and the* ASSISTANTS *swarm in to collect swords and flags from the battered actors.*

MAX, *calling up to* MAGGIE, *at mast.*   All right, we've got that scene. You don't have to go down with the ship.

MAGGIE.   Oh, I don't know. I've grown fond of the old tub. Why don't we take another twenty minutes and make *Moby Dick?*

MAX.   All the dead pirates get into new costumes! We have one more scene to do.

An ACTOR *comes to* MAX, *disgruntled.*

ACTOR.   Do I have to wear this beard? It hides my face.

MAX.   We're ahead. Look. You're Blackbeard the pirate. You've just scuttled five ships and you're landing on the island with your treasure and your captive women.

To ANDY, *who is hurrying through.*

How about the treasure chest?

ANDY.   All ready.

ACTOR.   Do I get a chance to act or am I just jumping around again?

MAX.   It's *your* scene! You discover the woman—Maggie. With one glance, you win her. She's finally met her mate.

MAGGIE, *coming down from the ship, hears the last of this.*

MAGGIE.   Max, wait a minute! Wait a minute! I've got a brainstorm. You're missing something great!

MAX.   What?

MAGGIE.   You're just going from one scene of violence to another scene of violence! That's wrong! Look. She's killed all the pirates. Then what?

MAX.   She gets a good night's rest.

MAGGIE.   No, no, no, you're not thinking! Hold everybody!
I've got to show you!

MAGGIE *runs into the lighthouse.* MAX *watches her go, a
satisfied glint in his eye.* PETE *and* BESSIE *enter, arms
folded, advancing on* MAX.

PETE.   Dreamer boy. Come here and listen. Okay?

BESSIE.   This is the Emergency Committee speaking.

PETE.   That Indian sequence. What year would you say it
took place in?

MAX.   Oh, about 1780.

PETE.   Well, nobody's been paid since.

BESSIE.   And furthermore, three of the pirates have rickets.

PETE.   Now you've been giving all your attention to our leading lady. So we've taken steps.

MAX.   Good. What steps?

BESSIE.   Simple. We asked ourselves, did we know anybody
with money?

PETE.   And we did.

BESSIE.   George.

PETE.   Good old George.

MAX.   Oh. Have you talked to him?

PETE.   He's arriving this afternoon with the payroll up to date. We told him to bring it in small bills.

MAX.   You're a credit to the organization. One thing, how long before he gets here?

BESSIE.   We don't know. I'll post a lookout.

BESSIE *off.*

PETE.   What difference does it make?

MAX.   I need a few minutes alone with Miss Harris.

PETE.   Oh.

MAX.   I have a feeling she's bursting to tell me something. And not about the picture.

PETE.   You mean like she's crazy about you?

MAX.   Let's not exaggerate.

PETE.   Max, she's not as tough as she seems. Let her go.

MAX.   No, dammit! She told me I wasn't worth stepping on. She's going to take it all back, and then some, before I point out the lesson for the day—never tangle with a low, common hustler.

PETE.   You watch your step.

MAGGIE *bustles out of lighthouse with a laundry basket full of window curtains, pillows, and flowerpots.* PETE *goes.*

MAGGIE. Don't look, Max! Please, don't look for just two seconds. This woman is stranded on the island. So where would she make a little home? Right here . . . see?

MAX, *turns to see that* MAGGIE *has decorated the ship with her props, making it look thoroughly domestic.* Well, I *like* the house. Of course, there's no garage——

MAGGIE. Don't you get it? It's Robinson Crusoe, only this time it's a woman. We get shots of her spearing fish and climbing for coconuts, and there's a little monkey that's a companion for the baby—

Darting all over and acting it out, enthusiastically.

—and we do a big hurricane thing, where it looks like the house is going to slide right into the ocean, but she lives through it all. And the next morning, when it finally clears, she sees footprints—right in front of her door. And she follows the footprints along until the footprints stop—and then she looks up——

Acting it out tensely, she has arrived at MAX. *As she looks up, there is a split second's silence. Something happens between them.* MAX *reaches out and kisses her. She does not resist. After the kiss there is a pause before* MAGGIE *speaks.*

Max, there's something I'd better tell you. I think I'm in love with you.

MAX *says nothing.*

Don't you have anything to tell me?

MAX *pauses, as though savoring the moment, turns away to ready himself for his little speech, turns back to face her.*

What?

*Then—without knowing quite what has hit him—*MAX *finds himself kissing* MAGGIE *again, ardently. Suddenly* MAGGIE *pulls out of it.*

Max! What am I going to tell George?

MAX.   George?

Vaguely, then remembering.

Wait a minute.

In a panic, calling off.

Pete!

Hastily, to MAGGIE.

There's something I've got to clear up.

At the same moment PETE *enters, jubilant, carrying a bulging satchel. He is followed by* BESSIE. ANDY *is coming on opposite.*

PETE.   It's here. Andy! Get everybody! Harvest time!

Tosses satchel to ANDY *before* MAX *can reach him.*

MAX.   Pete, no . . . no . . .

ANDY, *catching satchel.*   What is it?

BESSIE.   Cash!

MAX, *to* PETE, *desperately.*   I don't want his money! I don't want him here!

But GEORGE *is already with us.*

GEORGE.   Maggie! I came as soon as I could——

MAGGIE, *startled*.   George! What are you doing here?

GEORGE.   I came with the money.

MAGGIE.   The money?

The COMPANY *has swarmed in above and is being paid off. All are in high spirits.*

GEORGE.   They told me how good you were in the picture, and how they couldn't finish it without——

MAGGIE, *walking slowly toward* MAX.   They asked you for money?

GEORGE.   It's just a loan. I'll get it back as soon as they finish the Egyptian sequence. . . .

MAX, *it has all gone too fast*.   Maggie, listen——

ANDY, *running down to drag* GEORGE *up to the group being paid off*.   I want you to meet our friend and benefactor— George Randolph——

He is drowned out by cheers from the COMPANY.

MAX, *desperately to* MAGGIE.   I *know* what this looks like——

MAGGIE.   Yeah, but think of a smart kid like me falling for it! The most co-operative little meal ticket you ever made a pass at!

MAX.   *I* didn't ask George for the money!

MAGGIE, *furious sarcasm.* You didn't know anything about
it——

MAX. Yes, I *knew* about it, but——

MAGGIE. How about that sob story in the bar? You meant
every word of it.

MAX. No, no, I didn't——

MAGGIE. And when I finally fell into your arms you even had
that planned . . . !

PETE, *grabbing the camera and nudging* MAX *as he sees that*
GEORGE *is beginning to notice the quarrel.* Max, break it
up! He'll hear you.

MAX, *paying no attention to* PETE. Yes, yes, it *started* that
way! But now *listen!*

GEORGE, *on his way over to them.* Maggie, what's the matter?

PETE, *quickly taking* GEORGE's *arm and pulling him away.*
Mr. Brown, we're starting now.

Shouting to deflect attention.

Company, places!

COMPANY *immediately falls into place for Blackbeard
sequence.*

MAGGIE, *screaming at* MAX *over this.* Listen? Why should I
listen? You're not even a human being. All you care about
is your rotten picture! All right! Go ahead and finish it! But
you can finish it without me!

MAGGIE *runs wildly off, breaking her way through the crowd.* MAX *takes a few steps after her, furious, then signals bitterly to two members of the* COMPANY.

MAX.   All right. I'll finish my rotten picture, but I'll finish it *with* you. Get her! She's in this scene! Get her!

Striding to camera.

Begin!

As the two men go after MAGGIE, *the Pirate Orgy erupts. In a danced form, with the* PIRATES *shouting victoriously and singing a nonsense refrain, we see* BLACKBEARD *and his men spearing the male captives they have brought to the island. One* PIRATE *loses his grip on his man and* BLACK-BEARD *shouts:*

ACTOR.   Butterfingers! To the sharks!

All male captives are hurled to the sharks. A treasure chest is hauled on and plundered. Women captives are dragged in by the hair. In the midst of all this the two MEN *who have gone after* MAGGIE *break through the melee with* MAGGIE, *kicking and screaming, over their shoulders. She is dumped to her feet near* BLACKBEARD *and held firm in the scene.*

MAX.   Welcome home!

Trying to direct the scene as planned.

You look into Blackbeard's eyes.

MAGGIE *twists her head the other way.* BLACKBEARD's *hand reaches out and forces her to face him.*

A change comes over you. Love is born.

MAGGIE *spits at* BLACKBEARD, *furiously tries to wrench her-self free.*

MAGGIE.   Let me go! Let me go!

She nearly breaks loose in a lunge toward MAX.

MAX, *almost without skipping a beat, switches gears.*   Wait! This is better! We're changing the plot—she's a hellcat and has to be tamed! Tame her!

A roar goes up from the COMPANY. MAGGIE *does bolt free of* BLACKBEARD *in an effort to get at* MAX, *but* MAX *spins her around and hurls her back into the fray.*

Get back in there! You're wonderful!

GEORGE, *alarmed at what seems to be going on, plunges into the battle to rescue* MAGGIE, *but he is immediately set upon by four or five* PIRATES *and knocked to the ground.* LOIS *screams.*

LOIS.   George is hurt! George is hurt!

She is whisked out of the scene by two PIRATES. MAX *goes right on directing.*

MAX.   Hang onto her! Get her to the mast!

MAGGIE *is lifted, kicking wildly, into the air and forcibly thrown onto the deck of the ship, where* BLACKBEARD *is now waiting for her.*

Tie her up!

MAGGIE *is lashed to the mast.* PETE, *with camera, has been hoisted onto the shoulders of several* ASSISTANTS *and is rid-*

ing in toward the ship, cranking away. MAX, *on another pair of shoulders, follows, calling out commands as* PETE *and camera move in for a close-up of* MAGGIE. *The close-up must be something fierce:* MAGGIE *is hurling all the insults she can think of directly into the lens. The* PIRATES *are dancing in uncontrolled abandon as the curtain falls.*

END OF ACT I

ACT II

Scene 1

A pleasantly nautical double bedroom in a Home for Disabled Seamen. It is on the mainland, looking directly across the water toward Huckleberry Island and its lighthouse. Sitting up in one bed is GEORGE, *comfortable in his dressing gown; he has been brought here after the free-for-all on the island. On a night table at the head of the bed is a champagne bucket containing an opened bottle. On the other side of the room, sitting on the edge of a second bed, is* LOIS, *sipping champagne. Four* NURSES *are hovering over* GEORGE, *one of whom is taking his temperature. The* NURSES *are singing a light madrigal in unctuously sympathetic hospital tones.*

NURSES. Are we feeling any better?
  Are we sitting up today?
  Are we feeling gay—
  Merrier than May?

  Are the bruises and contusions
  We encountered in the fray
  Vanishing away today?

  Do be careful,
  Do be careful,

Mustn't overdo.
Do as doctor tells us
And we'll be as good as new.
Mustn't overdo,
Do as doctor tells us to.

GEORGE, *whipping the thermometer out of his mouth.* You
are not going to take my temperature one more time today!

LOIS. He's running a temperature from all the temperatures.

GEORGE. I am not sick, I have a slightly fractured collarbone,
I am getting out of here this afternoon——

LOIS, *as the* NURSES *retire.* Where do you suppose Maggie
can ever be?

GEORGE. I don't know. I've been here two days, the wedding
is supposed to be tomorrow, she hasn't come, she hasn't
called——

LOIS. I think it was very brave the way you tried to help her.
I wish somebody would do something dashing and romantic for me.

GEORGE, *studying her curiously, and smiling.* What's your
idea of romantic?

LOIS. Well, when I was a kid I used to think there were two
kinds of men. Men like my father and my uncle who wore
navy-blue pants and suspenders—and real men, gentlemen,
like you see in the better movies. Sheiks who carry titled
ladies off into the desert, and princes who dance with com-
moners and wear ribbons catty-corner across their chests. I

thought I'd meet them when I grew up. But where are they? All the men are like my uncle.

GEORGE. Wait a minute. It's not a red uniform that makes a man romantic. It's a girl that makes a man romantic.

LOIS. I'm a girl. Why don't I?

GEORGE. Lois, I hate to say this, but I've been watching you. I think you spoil your own chances—by being too eager, too available. You could meet the Prisoner of Zenda and you'd be chasing after coffee for him.

LOIS. No, sir! If I met any princes, they'd appreciate me.

GEORGE. Perhaps they already appreciate *other* ladies—ladies who don't try so hard.

LOIS. Oh, no. They're all starved for affection.

Sitting near him and sighing.

Why don't they find me?

She sings.

When I've had much too much to dream
And I seem
Pleasantly tipsy,
Pretenders plot and princes scheme,
All for love of a lady like me.

Polite hussars and brave dragoons,
Whole platoons,
Duel for my favor
While pale composers spin their tunes,
All for love of a lady like me.

Lady in waiting, patiently waiting,
Waiting for someone to fetch and to carry me
Ever so lightly, holding me tightly,
Into the night where he might even marry me—

I chase the boys who make me cry.

GEORGE. Why, oh, why?

LOIS. Genuine gentlemen
Seem to be in short supply.

GEORGE. Stuff and nonsense and fiddle-de-dee!

LOIS. I wish I could turn back the almanac.
I'd chase the gents and they'd chase me back,
I'd go off my trolley for Sir Walter Raleigh
And Raleigh'd rally round——

GEORGE. I wish I could make the directions plain.
You don't say, "Tarzan," till he says, "Jane."
Let him play the sheik, you play hide and go seek.
You have got to get lost to be found.

LOIS. Well, if I've had a dream or two,
Just a few, maybe too many,
I shan't swear off till one comes true,
Till there's love for a lady like me.

The room dissolves as a handsome GRENADIER *appears in
response to* LOIS' *yearning. Just as obediently a swarm of
poets, sheiks, and other romantic figures sweeps into view.*
LOIS *dances her fantasy of what her life will be like when
she meets the right sort of gentlemen, all of whom adore
her. The dream does not last.* GEORGE *watches and listens*

*from the edge of his bed in the shadows, and his warning
proves to be right: there are other women, more gracious
and enchanting than* LOIS, *and they draw all of* LOIS' *admirers away.* LOIS *puts up a game fight, tagging along and
doing her best to assert herself, but in the end she is left
alone—except for* GEORGE. *Ruefully, she acknowledges that
she has learned the lesson* GEORGE *has been trying to teach
her—that she must really become a lady in waiting.*

LOIS, *singing.* I'll wait till all the stars have set——

GEORGE. Wanna bet?

LOIS. Wait for my gentleman——

GEORGE. Dear, you've never waited yet——

LOIS. Stuff and nonsense and fiddle-de-dee.

Raising her champagne glass as the NURSES *return, carrying
flowers and singing a little obbligato against* LOIS' *last
refrain.*

Well, here's to dreams that might come true——

NURSES. Are we feeling any better?
Are we feeling any better?

GEORGE, *raising his glass.* Here's to you, you and your
gentleman——

NURSES. We must do what doctor tells us,
We must do what doctor tells us——

LOIS. Here's to fun until they do——

NURSES. Do be careful,
  Do be careful,
  Mustn't overdo.

LOIS. —fall in love with a lady like me.

GEORGE, *staring at her.* Fall in love with a lady like you.

NURSES. Yes, he's feeling better,
  Feeling better,
  Feeling mighty fine.

  GEORGE *takes the flowers from the* NURSES *and hands them to* LOIS, *smiling. The* NURSES *are leaving as the song ends and the room returns to normal.* MAGGIE *enters, swiftly and with obvious determination, going directly to the bed at the opposite side of the room.*

LOIS, *getting up quickly.* Well, it's high time you came to see our poor broken robin!

  She picks up her cloak and gets ready to go as MAGGIE *pops into the other bed.*

  And you won't need me.

  LOIS *slips out.*

GEORGE. Maggie, what are you doing?

  No answer.

  Maggie, get up! What will people think?

MAGGIE, *pulling covers up around her.* They'll think the worst. But if you don't have a baby in nine months, it'll all blow over.

GEORGE.   Where have you been?

MAGGIE.   I've been calming down.

GEORGE.   You don't look it.

MAGGIE.   I have decided on a plan of inaction. I'm going to
stay here, I'm not going to get up, I'm not going to marry
you, I'm not going to do *anything* until you get us both out
of Grady's clutches.

GEORGE.   All Grady wanted to do was complete the picture——

MAGGIE.   Picture? That's not a picture. That's a tapeworm.

GEORGE.   No, when I gave him the money he was only talking
about one more sequence. He was going to take the woman
back to ancient Egypt.

MAGGIE.   Well, he's not going to take *this* woman back to ancient Egypt!

GEORGE.   You see, Maggie, Grady is a dedicated man. His
methods may be somewhat questionable, but he believes
in what he's doing. I respect a man like that.

MAGGIE, *staring at him, aghast*.   You are! You are! You're taking his side!

She sings.

To the naked eye you're absolutely peerless,
You're brawny, brainy, fearless,
And you know what you're about.

And I tell myself you're such a manly specimen,
No matter what a mess I'm in
You'll surely get me out.
But would you?

MAGGIE *throws back the covers, gets to her feet, and advances on* GEORGE.

Or have I misunderstood you?
When I'm in a crisis
And ask what your advice is
Do you know what you'd answer?
Do you know what you'd do?

The scene is darkest Africa,
The water's nice and hot,
The cannibals have got me
Salt and peppered for the pot.
Then you coming running to the fray
And this is what you say:

Spoken. "But, dearest, cannibals have rights just like
other people!"

That's what you'd do, that's exactly what you'd do!
Where is the beast in you?

A pair of savage bloodhounds are
A-thirsting for the kill.
If one dog fails to eat me up
The other surely will
They're gaining fast, with open jaws,
You enter—and we pause——

Spoken. "Darling, what did you do to *provoke* these
dogs?"

That's what you'd do, that is exactly what you'd do!
Where is the beast in you?

I don't ask for a high-minded hero
As fair and understanding as can be,
Always ready to pursue
The other fellow's point of view,
Always searching for the truth to set us free!
He's a liberal? Well, dandy!
It's just that I demand he be

Spoken. A narrow-minded, small-horizoned, partisan, opinionated, bigoted, reactionary mule—

When it comes to me!

I'm huddled on the doorstep
And I cannot pay the rent.
The landlord with the mustache is
An evil, leering gent,
But through the blinding snow you come
To tell your little chum,

Spoken. "Tenants never *do* understand these things.
It costs *money* to run an apartment!"

That's what you'd do, that's exactly what you'd do!
Where, oh, where is the beast in you?

MAGGIE *pops back into bed and goes right on talking.*

All right. You let the picture go on, and I settle down here for the winter. It'll be a great place to spend Christmas, but——

GEORGE, *suddenly.* Maggie, do you love me?

MAGGIE, *caught off base, after a pause.* Would you marry me if I didn't love you?

The conversation is interrupted by the arrival of J.C., *pushed on in his wheel chair and flanked by* ACCOUNTANTS.

MAGGIE *immediately directs her attention to* J.C., *glad for the interruption, rattling on.*

I'm sorry. This bed is taken. Come any time, though. We're always in. You know, George, a little paint and paper will do wonders for this place. We were lucky to get it. It has that died-in feeling.

Meanwhile J.C. *has presented a portfolio and various ledgers to* GEORGE, *who is studying them.*

Don't bother to introduce me to your friend. Wait'll you see *my* relatives.

GEORGE *now hands* J.C. *a check, and* MAGGIE *notices.*

You think I'm not serious. You think at gun-point I'd go back. You think if I was starving and you were starving and your whole family was living on peanut-butter sandwiches, I'd go back.

J.C. *is now being wheeled out.*

Goodbye. Awfully nice seeing you.

Reverting to GEORGE.

But I tell you this. Not *your* blue eyes—or my soft head— or two million dollars—*nothing* is going to make me——

GEORGE, *interrupting the flow by handing her the portfolio he has received from* J.C. Here.

MAGGIE, *staring at it.* What is it?

GEORGE. It's a wedding present.

MAGGIE. Oh. And I was expecting roller skates. What is it?

GEORGE.   It's the picture. I bought it—lock, stock and camera
—from the man in the wheel chair.

MAGGIE, *exploding.   I* don't want that picture. What do I
want with the picture?

GEORGE, *cutting in quietly.*   You are now Grady's boss.

*Absolute silence. Her mouth drops open as the idea gets
through. He waits a second before he speaks.*

Grady doesn't know. Would you like me to tell him?

MAGGIE, *a fiendish look coming into her eyes.*   No. No, I
think it would come better from me!

GEORGE, *watching her closely as she gets out of bed.*   He's up
in the country at Bessie's place. But you don't really ever
have to see him again. From the look of these books, you
can put him in jail.

MAGGIE.   But would that be enough?

Having kissed him, she heads for the door.

GEORGE.   What do you plan to do?

MAGGIE.   Just open the windows. You'll hear.

GEORGE *looks after her a moment, speculatively, then sings.*

GEORGE.   I can't deny that you're in love
If love is blind.
With half an eye you would have seen
That kiss was kind.

If you grew tired of me
You'd tell me so—
But you would clearly be
The last to know.

Shall I take my heart and go, my love?
Would you ever even know, my love?
Can't you see, my darling, what a tangled web we weave
When we make believe we care?
If I simply said goodbye, my love,
Would you even wonder why, my love?
Though a dream lies dying
I'm the only one who's crying—
Dear, if I should wander
Would your heart grow fonder?
Shall I take my heart and go?

NURSES *bring* GEORGE's *clothes to him.*

NURSE 1.   Dr. King says you may go any time now. Isn't that splendid?

GEORGE, *musing about* MAGGIE, *as he changes from his dressing gown.*   Yes.

NURSE 2.   Your friend was certainly happy to see you better.

GEORGE.   Hm?

NURSE 3.   She was so gloomy when she came, and so cheerful when she left!

GEORGE, *abstracted.*   Yes.

NURSES *bustle off.*

GEORGE, *sings.*   If I simply said goodbye, my love,
Would you even wonder why, my love?
Though a dream lies dying
I'm the only one who's crying.
Dear, if I should wander
Would your heart grow fonder?
Shall I take my heart and go?

The lights fade.

Scene 2

At BESSIE'S *barn, a fairish way up the Hudson. The two-story barn is at left, surrounded by greenery. Below it stands a boxcar, half hidden by the foliage—it is on a single-track railroad spur that passes the barn and runs down to join the main line off left.* BESSIE'S *house is barely visible upstage. At opening,* ANDY *is on top of the boxcar, waving off left to other* ASSISTANTS.

ANDY.   Okay! We're all loaded here! How about you?

VOICE, *off.*   All set! We can lock 'em up!

ANDY, *calling as he starts to come down the ladder on the side of the car.*   Bessie!

1ST ASST. *comes out of the barn.*

1ST ASST.   Nothing left in the barn!

He leaves, along the line of boxcars.

BESSIE, *coming down the path from her house.*   What do you want?

ANDY.   Will you tell Mr. Grady we're ready to go?

BESSIE.   Sure.

ANDY.   And we cleaned out the barn, Bessie. It's all yours again!

BESSIE.   Thanks, but I hate that barn. And I'll tell you why. You know how people always ask, "What's the matter, were you born in a barn?" I never know what to say. I was born in that barn.

BESSIE *returns to the house. Before* ANDY *can leave,* MAGGIE *enters, the portfolio under her arm.*

ANDY, *surprised.*   Hi, Miss Harris.

MAGGIE.   Hi, Andy.

ANDY.   Didn't expect to see you here today.

MAGGIE.   What are you doing—making a railroad picture?

ANDY.   No, ma'am. We're going to California.

MAGGIE, *eyebrows up.*   Oh?

ANDY, *proudly and innocently.*   You know what's in these boxcars? Every bit of our Egyptian scenery.

MAGGIE, *pleasantly, playing him along.*   All sixteen thousand dollars' worth?

ANDY.   Eighteen thousand now! We're going to hook the cars onto the five-thirty train.

MAGGIE.   What are you going to California for?

ANDY.   Mr. Grady says the weather's better. But that's not the real reason. We have to get the scenery out of the state.

MAGGIE.   Oh? Why?

ANDY.   We got word that J.C. is selling out to some sucker. But what this poor sap doesn't know is there's nothing to buy. We're taking it all with us.

MAGGIE.   Say, that's clever!

ANDY.   Oh, nobody gets the jump on Max Grady!

MAGGIE.   I know. He's one of the great thinkers of our time. *Suddenly.*

Andy, I've never seen one piece of that Egyptian scenery.

As 2ND ASST. *comes through carrying Egyptian costumes.*

Is it all right if I take a little peek?

ANDY.   Sure. Sam, open up some of those cars and show Miss Harris.

2ND ASST. *nods pleasantly and takes* MAGGIE *off left.* BESSIE *reappears from house.*

BESSIE.   Andy, Max is packing his suitcase. He'll be right with you.

PETE *hurries on, carrying a suitcase and dressed for travel.*

PETE.   Are we all ready?

BESSIE, *looking him over.*   I like that suit. That's how much *I* know.

MAX *bristles down the lane from the house, carrying a bulging and unlocked suitcase. He is obviously rattled about something.*

MAX.   Bessie, *I* can't shut this suitcase! Here—you're stronger than I am. Andy, I forgot my sweater. I think you'll find it under the cat.

ANDY *runs up to the house.* PETE, *staring back at* MAX, *goes off toward boxcars.*

BESSIE, *working over* MAX'S *suitcase and hauling out a single high-button shoe.*   Max, what's this?

MAX.   I always thought it was a shoe. What does it look like to you?

BESSIE.   Yeah, but where's the other one?

MAX, *fidgeting.*   How do I know?

BESSIE.   Well, you can always plant it with philodendron.

MAX, *nerving himself to say what is on his mind.*   Say, Bessie —if I didn't go on this train, would the boys think it was funny?

BESSIE, *sizing him up, shrewdly.*   If you're going to walk, you'd better have both shoes.

MAX, *rationalizing.*   I could go into town, clean up a few business matters, and take a later train——

BESSIE.   What business? Maggie?

MAX, *caught, and turning away.*   Forget it.

BESSIE.   I'm sorry you're going. We could have made beautiful money together.

MAX, *tenderly, if abstracted.*   Thanks, Bessie. Thanks for everything.

BESSIE.   You're welcome. And Max. One other thing.
He turns to her.
The rent.

MAX.   Bessie, I want you to have this—
Fishing a curio out of his pocket.
—my good luck charm. It's a boar's tooth.

BESSIE.   I'll keep it always. I certainly won't be able to give it away.
Watches MAX, who is pacing nervously.
Max, if you want to go back to town to see Maggie, you go back and see her.

MAX, *jumping.*   Who wants to see her? I don't want to see her!

BESSIE.   I know what you need. I'll go up to the kitchen and make you a nice hot cup of gin.

BESSIE *goes to the house.* MAX, *furious with himself, sings.*

MAX.   I can't be in love, I can't be in love!
  You can see that I'm
  (a) unstable
  (b) unable
  (c) unprepared to marry her or any other.
  It's an inconvenient time and furthermore I'm much too
      young to leave my mother.

  I can't be in love, I can't be in love!
  It's apparent I'm
  (a) too risky
  (b) too frisky
  (c) just a guy of unreliable libido.
  I am sure to stray and anyway I simply do not own a good
      tuxedo.

  Yes, she's sweet, yes, she's clever,
  I admit I could sit and look in her eyes, her beautiful eyes,
      forever—
  Never!
  I can't be in love, I can't be in love!
  For the record I'm
  (a) unsteady
  (b) unready
  (c) unavailable in certain busy seasons.
  I am poor and immature and unemployed and then besides
      I have my reasons!

  You see before you a man who had his life all planned—
  Who wandered down love's highway hand in hand in hand
      in hand in hand in hand.
  Asking little, taking all,
  Brunettes in summer, blondes in fall.
  Now look at me—
  Slain, slain, slain!

By the nearest smile, the merest smile, the dearest smile
That ever drove a roving man insane!

I can't be in love, I can't be in love!
For the record I'm
(a) neurotic
(b) quixotic
(c) idiotically inclined to cutting capers.
I'm a ne'er-do-well and sure as hell I'd never learn to share
the morning papers.

I can't be in love, I can't be in love!
Matrimony is
(a) too sticky
(b) too tricky
(c) I believe I'll leave the lions' den to Daniel.
Any time that I get lonely I have only got to get a cocker
spaniel.

Yes, she's sweet, yes, she's clever,
I admit I could sit and look in her eyes, her beautiful eyes,
forever—
Never!
I can't be in love, I can't be in love!
Heaven knows I've been
'Round a-plenty,
Clowned a-plenty,
Found lovers' lane a most enchanting place to visit.
Now I want to plant my feet there, there's a girl I want to
meet there that I wouldn't dare to cheat there. If this
caring isn't really love, what is it?
I can't be . . . can't be . . . can't be in love . . .
Could I?

MAX *has turned away to struggle with the suitcase when*
MAGGIE *appears behind him.*

MAGGIE, *sweetly*.   Hello, Max.

MAX, *jumps*.   Maggie! Where did you come from? Look—you
wouldn't listen to me on the island, but I do want to explain——

MAGGIE, *eluding him, and purring mysteriously*.   Max, you
don't have to explain anything to me! After all, we've had
a lot of fun together—we're adults——

BESSIE *returns with a plate of nut bread*.

BESSIE.   Max, I've fixed you a little treat! I made some of my
date-nut bread.

MAGGIE.   Hello, Bessie.

BESSIE.   Oh, hello, dear. Will you see that he eats some of this?

A hint.

I haven't been able to get him to touch anything for two
days.

BESSIE *goes*.

MAGGIE, *very domestically, while MAX stands baffled*.   Max,
you've got to eat some of this! You'll hurt Bessie's feelings.

Nibbling at some herself.

And it's good.

He is bewildered and beginning to be suspicious.

Don't look so puzzled. You didn't expect me to stay mad
forever, did you? Really, it all seems pretty funny now. I
keep seeing myself being hauled up to that mast——

Laughing, then a sudden crunch on the date-nut bread.
Ooh!

MAX.   What?

MAGGIE.   Bessie has a brand-new slant on date-nut bread.
You leave in the shells. Or else my tooth is having a tooth.
Chattily.
You know, this is all your fault. I was supposed to go to
the dentist the day I started "Frontier Woman."

PETE *comes from the line of boxcars, urgently, looking at
his watch.*

PETE.   It's five-fifteen. We've got to get moving.

MAGGIE.   By golly, he's right! Here—don't forget your suitcase.

MAX, *following her.*   Maggie! Will you *stop* whatever you're
doing?

MAGGIE, *innocently.*   What's the matter? I just came to say
goodbye and wish you luck.

PETE, *calling to* ASSISTANTS.   Okay, boys! Roll 'em down!

ASSISTANTS *begin to roll the visible boxcar away.*

MAGGIE, *politely.*   Oh, excuse me. What are you doing?
They stop and look at her.

I know you're going to California—but you hadn't planned
to take my scenery?

PETE.   Your scenery?

MAGGIE.   Yes. Actually, I didn't *want* the scenery, but George
is so sentimental—he thought it would be something for me
to play with. He gave it to me as a wedding present.

She turns and smiles at MAX.

Of course, you don't have to take *my* word for it——

She hands MAX *the portfolio.*

MAX, *tossing it away without looking at it.*   All right. Where
do we go from here?

The others steal away, quietly.

MAGGIE.   Well, now, that's a real question, Max. I've been
thinking about this picture. Do you know what's the matter with it? It's not long enough. All because you want to
jump from that pirate girl way back to Egypt. What about
the golden years between? Surely that pirate had a grandmother? She didn't come from an egg! You've hit on a hot
thing, Max, and you're letting it slip through your fingers.
Think about it. Have we been fair to Islam? I think wher-
ever you hit a grandmother, there's your scene! Now these
are only suggestions, mind you, but why don't you consider
them—because, after all, *you* are working for *me!*

MAX, *glancing at his watch and turning to go.*   Not as of five-
seventeen today.

MAGGIE. All right, you give me no alternative. I'll scrap the film and I can probably sell those silly idols to some amusement park.

MAX, *stopping and turning on her.* You wouldn't.

MAGGIE. Yes, I would. After all, I'm going to be Mrs. George Randolph Brown and I shouldn't be on display in these cheap nickel theaters anyway——

MAX, *an explosion.* Shut up! Shut your big, superior mouth. Where did you get to be so damned almighty? You've been walking around here holding your nose since the day you came and if you want to patronize me, all right. But let me tell you something. You know who likes these five-cent pictures? People—ordinary, dumb, stupid, honest-to-God people. You think I make these pictures to steal a buck, don't you? Do you want to know why I make them? Because I like to go into these cheap nickel theaters, sit next to those nuts, and watch them have one hell of a time! You think they're wrong, don't you? But do you know what? This picture is better than the last one, and the last one was better than the one before that, and the next one might even be good if I had someone who just ten-percent believed it! You know what I think is cheap? I think slumming is cheap. I think not doing your job is cheap. You're supposed to be an actress, but you sure as hell don't talk like one. Scrap the film—sell the scenery! My advice to you, kid, is to go into sand and gravel and leave this business to the pros.

MAX *walks out on her. She is visibly shaken by his outburst.* PETE *returns apprehensively.*

PETE. Miss Harris—what do you want us to do about the scenery? Unload it?

MAGGIE, *vaguely, rattled, not looking at him.*   I—I'm really
going to be very busy, Pete—I'm late now for a party at the
Browns'—and since we're going to Europe on our honey-
moon——

Sudden decision.

Tell Grady he can have it.

Abruptly, and not wanting to talk further, she goes.

PETE, *shouting to the others, off.*   Hey!

BESSIE, ANDY, 1ST ASST., 2ND ASST. *run in as* PETE *grabs portfolio, waves it.*

ANDY.   What?

PETE.   It's ours! We don't have to go to California! We can
set it up in the cornfield and shoot it tomorrow.

Cheers from the others as they gather about the portfolio.

ANDY, *to* 2ND ASST.   Go and tell Mr. Grady.

2ND ASST., *off, fast.*

1ST ASST.   How did you do it?

PETE.   I wish I knew, so I could do it again.

ANDY.   Mr. Grady will be proud!

1ST ASST.   I hope he appreciates all we do for him.

PETE.   He needs us. Crooked as he is, he needs us.

They sing.

Who has a rendezvous with destiny?
Who blazes trails ne'er blazed before?
Who does? He with the derring-do does!
I give you our founder—rotten to the core!

Why should he have a reserved seat in the parlor car
While you have to move to the back of the bus?
What has he got that you haven't got?
He's got us!

His little old bad companions!
Remember that the best are none too bad—
When you're in jail there is no doubt
You need a pal to help you out,
You need your bad, bad, bad companions.

It's been that way all through history—

PETE.   It's known that Jesse James could shoot
But did you know he drank?
And who held good old Jesse up
While he held up the bank?

ALL.   It was his bad companions!
Remember that the best are none too bad—
When you swear off wine and song
You need a friend to set you wrong,
You need your bad, bad, bad companions.

PETE.   Genghis Khan was satisfied
To give his foes a trimmin'.
Who did the dreary routine work
Of ravishing the women?

ALL. It was his bad companions!
Remember that the best are none too bad—
When your wife runs off with a brand-new mate
You need a friend to celebrate,
You need your bad companions.

BESSIE. His mother called him Percival
When he was but a nipper.
Who broke him of his sissy ways
And made him Jack the Ripper?

ALL. It was his bad companions!
Remember that the best are none too bad—
When you've insured your lady love
You need a helping hand to shove,
You need your bad, bad, bad companions.

PETE. Agawak, the cannibal king,
Ate those whom he defeated.
Who went and got bicarbonate
Whenever they repeated?

ALL. It was his bad companions!

*They speak in unison, raising their hands in a sort of Boy
Scout oath that gradually turns into a claw.*

A good bad companion is lazy, shiftless, yellow, treach-
erous,
Corrupt, dirty, insubordinate, and always there when you
need him.

They sing.

When museums made of wax
Immortalize our gracious Max
Let no one minimize his fame.

He plays a dirty, filthy game
But it takes more than grit like his
To be the son of a b. that he is,
It takes his bad, bad, bad companions!

BLACKOUT

Scene 3

The scene begins in an anteroom at Ten Oaks, where a party following the wedding rehearsal is in progress. GEORGE'S *guests are dancing a one-step of the period, and* LOIS *is floating among them.* GEORGE *discovers her and smiles fondly.*

GEORGE.   Hello!

LOIS, *brightly*.   Hello! It was awfully nice of Maggie to invite me tonight. All I want to do is stay in this pretty dress in this pretty house—

GEORGE, *as various well-dressed guests pass* LOIS, *admiring her*.   —and watch all the gentlemen smile at you?

LOIS, *delighted*.   You know—they sort of are?

GUEST, *approaching* LOIS.   May I have this dance?

LOIS, *winking at* GEORGE, *letting him know that she's learned her lesson*.   Certainly.

GEORGE *grins as he watches her dance away. The anteroom now opens up to a full ballroom, where the* GUESTS *dance a Maxixe in the style of the period.* LOIS *is very much the center of attention.*

As the dance reaches a climax, we see MAGGIE *and* GEORGE *swirling through in each other's arms, though* MAGGIE'S *smile seems a bit forced.*

Suddenly MAGGIE *and* GEORGE *stop dead. They have come face to face with* MAX, *who has appeared, hat in hand, in the ballroom, decidedly not dressed for the occasion. All of the dancers stop, staring at him.*

MAGGIE, *under her breath.*   Max . . . !

GEORGE, *helping out.*   Why, hello there, Mr. Grady. It's nice to see you.

MAX.   Would you mind if I spoke to Maggie for one minute?

GEORGE, *glancing at* MAGGIE.   Not at all.

GEORGE *turns to leave.* LOIS *takes his arm and they walk slowly off,* GEORGE *looking back. Waltz music begins and the* GUESTS *dance away, leaving* MAX *and* MAGGIE *alone.*

MAGGIE.   How did you get past the butler?

MAX.   Maggie—I've got something to say.

MAGGIE.   You always did have.

MAX.   For two years the one thing I cared about was getting hold of that scenery. Today I got it.

MAGGIE.   Okay, I consider myself thanked.

She moves away.

MAX, *follows her.*   Now that I've got it, I realize there's something I want more.

Pause.

I'm in love with you.

Pause.

Say something.

MAGGIE.   Well, it's been a day of thrills, hasn't it?

MAX.   Never mind the wisecracks. I love you and I want to marry you. I think you love me.

MAGGIE, *bracing herself and facing him.*   No, Max. Whatever I feel for you, I've been through that revolving door and come out the other side. You see, once in a while I like to feel that things are on the level.

MAX.   Oh, do you?

MAGGIE.   Yes, I do.

MAX.   Then how do you explain your presence here?

MAGGIE.   What do you mean?

MAX.   You wouldn't dare tell me you're in love with George because I know better. You're getting ready to marry a very nice guy for no other reason than he happens to fit in with your idiot dream of yourself. I don't think that's being on the level. I think that's pretty shabby. And one of these days you're going to wake up with a very clear picture of what's happened to you, and I won't be around to hear about it.

He leaves. She almost takes a step after him.

MAGGIE.   Max!

Slowly MAGGIE *turns around to look at the empty ballroom. Then she moves toward us and sings.*

I knew on the day I met him
He wasn't the man for me,
I knew I should just forget him
But I had to wait and see.

Oh, I've been sad before
And I've been had before
But oh, my friend, I won't pretend
It was as bad before.
I should have told my heart to stop and count ten
Because I never know when to say when.

I know my way around,
I never play around,
Each time I fall I bet my all
He's gonna stay around.
It seems that everything is rosy and then
Somehow I never know when to say when.

But now I've learned my lesson
And it's an easy one:
You've got to keep them guessin'
Keep it fun
Kiss and run—

The skies are stormy now,
My dreams all bore me now,
No candle lights the lonely nights

That lie before me now.
I swear it's done, it's done, it's over—Amen!
But then again and again and again
I find I never know when,
I never know when to say when.

LOIS *enters to find* MAGGIE *crying.*

LOIS.   Maggie—!

MAGGIE, *sings to* LOIS.   But now I've learned my lesson
And it's an easy one——

LOIS.   What's the matter?

MAGGIE.   You've got to keep 'em guessin',
Keep it fun,
Kiss and run——

Speaks to LOIS *over music.*

Lois, will you do me a favor?

LOIS.   Sure, Maggie. What?

MAGGIE.   Will you find George? Tell him I'll talk to him in
a minute—and be nice to him, Lois. Will you do that for me?

LOIS *nods, looks sympathetically at* MAGGIE, *and goes.* MAG-
GIE *sings.*

The skies are stormy now,
My dreams all bore me now,
No candle lights the lonely nights
That lie before me now.
I swear it's done, it's done, it's over—Amen!

But then again and again and again
I find I never know when,
I never know when to say when.

The lights fade.

Scene 4

Just outside BESSIE's *cornfield. Dawn. The crew are returning from having set up Egypt.*

ANDY.   Hey, look! It's daylight. We worked all night!

1ST ASST.   What time is it?

2ND ASST.   Six A.M.

ANDY.   But she's up! Egypt in all her glory!

BESSIE.   Boys, I got coffee and pancakes in the kitchen!

1ST ASST.   Good. I'm frozen.

ANDY.   Oh, it'll warm up.

PETE, *to* BESSIE.   Have you been over to the cornfield to see Egypt?

BESSIE.   I saw it.

PETE.   What did you think?

BESSIE.   Well, I won't need a scarecrow this year.

MAX *enters, with a false heartiness.*

MAX.   Boys, I'm proud of you. We'll start shooting in half an hour.

PETE.   Max, you're not really going to use Lois?

MAX.   Why not?

PETE.   She's never acted in her life.

MAX.   We'll get her through somehow. I hope.

MAX *goes.*

ANDY, *to* PETE.   Gee, did you think this day would ever come?

PETE, *as members of* COMPANY *begin to straggle in, getting into Egyptian costume.*   Two long years—!

PETE, BESSIE, *and members of the* COMPANY *sing.*

ALL.   Two years in the making!
  Two years on the way!
  The picture they said could never be made
  Is gonna be made today.

  See it now—an epic theme!
  See it now—a daring first!
  Unforgettable
  Unsurpassed
  Unashamed
  Unrehearsed!

Torn between a mother's love—
Tempted by unbridled lust—
Bring the kiddies,
Fun for all,
It's amazing!
It's a must!

Two years in the making!
Two years on the way!
The picture they said could never be made
Is gonna be made today.

See inside Egyptian temples,
See what really goes on,
See alluring virgins with
Hardly any clothes on.

See the flaming idol eating
Maidens for a hobby,
See the idol eat them up—
Doctors in the lobby!

BESSIE.   Why is this one of the truly great films of our time?
PETE.   It is first of all a love story,
    A story of two lovers,
    In love with each other.
    A stolen kiss their only crime—
    A simple story of pagan joy.
BESSIE.   Not since "Mother Ferguson's Boy"
    Has there been such courage—
ALL.   Raw!
PETE.   Fury—
ALL.   Savage!
BESSIE.   Passion—
ALL.   Searing!
PETE.   Action—

ALL.   Pounding!
Churning—Pulsing—Thundering—Throbbing!
BESSIE.   And loaded with chuckles!

ALL.   Two years in the making!
Two years on the way!
The picture they said could never be made
Is gonna be made today.

EGYPT! EGYPT! E-G-Y-P-T!
See the camels
See the slave girls
See the handsome hero save girls
See the idol
See the oracle
Hysterical! Historical!

Two years in the making!
Two years on the way!
The picture they said could never be made
Is gonna be made today.

MAX *enters, is handed his megaphone, and goes to his director's chair.*

ALL.   And it's
Coming!
MAX.   Cast of thousands!
ALL.   Coming!
MAX.   Runs for minutes!
ALL.   An emotional typhoon!
Watch for it!
PETE.   Watch out for it!
ALL.   Coming! Coming to your neighborhood soon!

BLACKOUT

Scene 5

Egypt. The massive golden scenery recedes far into the distance. At the top of a flight of steps stands an openmouthed idol, flanked by massive, bare-chested GUARDS. *There is a shallow laving pool downstage. A riot of elephants, griffins, and assorted six-handed figures rises to the sky. As* MAX *directs, the* COMPANY *dances a sacrificial dance. A choral chant is heard in the background.*

COMPANY. Lovely heart of stone, you promised paradise,
How could I have known you told a thousand lovely lies?
Other loves than mine will flame and fade away,
Ashes at your shrine, poor dusty loves of yesterday.
Heart of stone, you are a devil with a face as fair as
    morning.
Give your heart away, for on the desert wind I hear a
    warning:
Time will find you where this bright pavilion stands, and
    leave no token,
Just a legend and, upon the sighing summer sands, a broken
Heart of stone.

Into the picture comes LOIS, *wearing a vast cape and an enormous headdress.* PETE *is photographing her entrance.*

Meanwhile, several unused members of the COMPANY *are huddled about a small coal stove, off set, overcoats pulled around them.*

MAX, *giving directions to* LOIS, *a trace of despair in his voice.* Keep coming! Up . . . up . . . up.

LOIS *is bodily lifted by* GUARDS *high up over the laving pool until she is standing before the idol. She lets out a little shriek along the way.*

You're a princess. You've come on a pilgrimage. There is a drought on the land. The crops have dried up, the cattle are dying. A terrible heat presses down over Egypt. You've come to beg the gods for help.

GUARDS *turn her to face the idol.*

You are now in the presence of the idol.

Pause as LOIS *stands there.*

Remove your sandals.

LOIS *promptly kicks off both sandals by flipping one to the right of her, the other to the left, without otherwise moving a muscle. A* GUARD *is slightly clipped by a sandal, the* OTHER *jumps away in time.* MAX *gets up out of his chair with a despairing sigh and crosses to* PETE.

I'm not going to kill her. I'm going to hire a man. They do it for fifty bucks and your troubles are over.

Shouting to ACTORS *who are huddled around the stove.*

Will you get the hell away from that stove and stand ready?

ACTOR.   It's cold.

MAX.   It is April 23.

ACTORS.   It's cold!

PETE, *beating his arms at the camera.*   It happens to be the coldest April 23 in fourteen years.

MAX, *as though washing his hands of the whole business.* Look, we'll just get a picture of her standing there. Shoot it.

Calling directions, but without hope.

Guards, step in to her.

They do.

Rip off her cloak.

With a great sweeping gesture, GUARD *gets* LOIS' *cloak at the shoulder and rips it away. Over a flimsy oriental costume,* LOIS *has on a big, baggy man's sweater with a huge H on it.* MAX *has just about given up the ghost.*

I don't really care, but what is that?

LOIS.   It's cold.

MAX.   Take it off.

LOIS *makes an upward gesture to show that the sweater obviously will not go over the headdress.*

LOIS.   I'll have to take off the headdress.

MAX.   Take off the headdress.

LOIS, *to* GUARDS.   Would you boys . . . ?

GUARDS *step in and remove her headdress, carrying it heavily away.* LOIS *now slips out of the sweater by pulling it down over her shoulders and stepping out of it.*

PETE, *to* MAX, *seriously.*   Hey. This is silly. Knock off for the day and we'll go find a girl.

MAX.   No, let's get it over with.

PETE, *gesturing at the scenery they've fought so hard for.* You're wasting all this!

MAX.   Okay. I'm wasting it! Pete, I'm through. I'm going to Florida and get rich.

PETE, *ready to plead again.*   Max——

MAX, *through his teeth, meaning* LOIS.   We'll just get her to do what she can do, and put "The End" on it.

ASSISTANT *hurries in with supply of hot coffee.*

ASSISTANT.   Hot coffee!

Great stir from the COMPANY, *diving for it.*

MAX.   Never mind the coffee. Get over here!

COMPANY *groans and huddles near steps in overcoats.*

You crawl up the steps.

LOIS *stands on one foot, like a crane, folds of her flimsy skirt pulled desperately around her.* MAX *glares at her and she straightens up.*

You beg the princess to offer sacrifice, to appease the gods.

Remember—you're baked, you're parched, you're running with sweat!

ASSISTANT, *starting down line of girls.*   Coats!

SLAVE GIRLS *reluctantly surrender their overcoats to* ASSISTANT *as he whips by. They stand there shivering in practically nothing at all.*

MAX, *with cameras starting.*   Men! Help the women up the steps. They're fainting. Joe—lower that girl to the steps.

ACTOR *does. As the* GIRL *touches the step she lets out a piercing squeal;* MAX *is livid, misunderstanding.*

Listen, wise guy, you pinch her one more time and—!

ACTOR.   I didn't touch her.

GIRL.   You take off *your* pants and sit on that concrete!

MAX.   Go on, just go on! Lois, you hear their pleas and you are going to intercede. Offer your baby. You're willing to sacrifice your baby.

SLAVES *hand her a baby, which she holds up before idol.*

Smoke.

Great puff of smoke comes out of idol's mouth. LOIS *coughs violently.*

That means the idol is not satisfied. He doesn't want your baby. He wants *you.* You have to cleanse yourself. Guards, take her down to the pool.

GUARDS *lead* LOIS *toward pool.*

LOIS, *while being led, eyes up in terror.* Not in the water! You're not going to put me in the water!

MAX. And I don't want to hear one more word about how cold it is! It is spring, it is the month of April, it is not that cold!

LOIS' *foot, stepping into the pool, cracks through a tinkle of ice.*

PETE, *singing to himself, cranking camera.* Jingle bells, jingle bells, jingle all the way——

MAX, *after a savage look at* PETE, *driving ahead.* Guards! Lift up the sacred vessels! Anoint her.

GUARDS *take up urns and pour a stream of water over* LOIS. *She lets out a piercing scream.*

Around to the stairway now! Up to the idol! Fans!

NUBIAN SLAVES *raise great feathered fans in the air and wave them at* LOIS *as she goes up steps. She nearly dies of the blast.*

Your courage fails. The idol means flaming death. You shriek in terror.

LOIS *does this as best she can.*

You struggle. Your prince breaks out of the crowd.

All of this is acted out swiftly; PRINCE *knocks down the* TWO GUARDS.

One guard! Two guards! You're free! Your prince has saved you!

PRINCE *throws his arms open wide. Instead of going to him,*

LOIS *suddenly scurries up the steps and tiptoes into the idol's mouth.* MAX *is in total despair.*

What did you do that for?

LOIS, *her head peering out through the smoke.* It's so nice and warm in here!

MAX *is turning away, a broken man.*

Maggie!

MAX *stops and freezes at what he sees.* GEORGE *and* MAGGIE *have entered together.*

MAX.   Excuse me. Aren't you two in the wrong parish?

GEORGE.   I asked Maggie to do me one last favor. To finish the picture.

MAX.   What do you mean—one last favor?

GEORGE, *philosophically, with a slight smile.* Well, we're going to have to send back an awful lot of salad bowls.

There is a pause as MAX *simply looks at* MAGGIE, *relief welling up in him. Then he quickly snatches her hand and whirls her across stage toward an exit.*

MAGGIE, *halting him.* What are you doing?

MAX.   I can't propose in front of the idol. I'm a Presbyterian.

MAGGIE, *struggling and freeing herself.* Max—I'm not going to marry you!

MAX.   We don't have to get really married. We'll find a neighborhood where they have liberal views and——

As MAGGIE *turns away.*

Maggie. We're two of a kind.

MAGGIE.   It would take a sign from heaven, Max, to make me marry you.

MAX.   It doesn't happen that way. You're making a mistake.

She shakes her head, admitting that that's true, but still stubborn.

COMPANY, *who have heard every word, fascinated.*   Yes!

MAX, *realizing they've listened, and just letting fly.*   You hear that? Nosy and stupid as they are, even *they* know you're making a mistake!

MAGGIE.   Can we go to work?

Stripping off her coat to reveal that she is already costumed and starting up steps toward idol, with a nod toward the camera.

Pete!

The other ACTORS *hesitantly move to shooting positions, looking wonderingly at* MAX.

MAX.   Oh, sure, you can start, Pete! Word has come down from on high! We can go right ahead! The Divine Sarah is with us.

LOIS, *coming down from the idol toward* MAX, *carrying her sweater.* You won't be wanting me—as usual?

MAX.   Oh, I think you ought to stick around here now, and pick up a few pointers. I'm sure we're going to have the performance of the century!

GEORGE *offers* LOIS *his coat. She smiles and snuggles into it.* MAX *goes right on, calling up at* MAGGIE, *who is acting the scene and doing it well.*

Are you trying to express an emotion, or is that tooth bothering you again?

MAGGIE, *while acting.*   I think you ought to make up your mind whether you want to be a dentist or a director.

MAX.   How come you haven't mentioned how cold it is? I'll tell you why. Because you haven't noticed. Because *you're* made of ice, that's why!

Crossing to GEORGE *and shaking his hand.*

George, you had a narrow escape.

Switching emotions.

Maggie—if I said *please*——

MAGGIE.   Max, you are making an idiot of yourself in front of the entire company!

MAX, *speaking to the* COMPANY *as they play the scene, with brisk, cold efficiency.*   All right, all right, let's wind this thing up! No matter what happens, for richer or poorer, in sickness and in health, we finish the picture today! Remember the heat—you're dying of the heat—you're hot. You're——

Slowly it begins to snow. MAX, *noticing it first, stops. Gradually the others notice and slowly raise their heads to the skies.* PETE *stops cranking the camera to look up. And* MAGGIE, *feeling it on her arms, stares around her, realizes what this means, and looks down at* MAX. *Then she laughs.*

MAGGIE.   Max—it's a sign! It's a sign!

MAX *bolts up the steps to her. They hold off for a tense second, then grab each other and are kissing furiously as the snow comes pouring down as though in an overturned paperweight.*

MUSIC.

CURTAIN